I want to dedicate this book to my precious daughter Mila Jamie. She is the most compassionate, kind and intelligent little girl that I have ever met. She loves animals and is so caring to animals and people. She is just six years old but she makes me incredibly proud. She lights up my world when days are dark. Thank you my little Angel. I hope that as you get older you see in me a dad who is a role model when it comes to how a man treats a woman.

I love you boatloads and know that it doesn't matter how old you are, you will always be my little girl and I will always cherish the day you were born and came into the lives of your mom and me.

Also by Mark Keohane

Chester
Springbok Rugby Uncovered
Champions of the World
Monty (Illustrated)
Monty

Bulletproof: The James Dalton Story
First published 2019

Highbury Media, 36 Old Mill Street, Ndabeni, 7405, Cape Town, South Africa

Editor: Zelim Nel
Design: Rashied Rahbeeni
Proofreader: Alan Valkenburg
Cover Photo: Gareth Van Nelson
Other photos: James Dalton collection, Gallo Images
Printer: CTP printers

ISBN 978-0-9870340-6-9.

ACKNOWLEDGEMENTS

I would like to thank Cullinan Holdings, specifically Michael Tollman for his trust and belief in me.

To the Cullinan family for their friendship and to all the Exco members.

I really also want to acknowledge and thank Claire for Mila.

To my parents for bringing me up. My dad is the best dad and only showed me kindness and love with the utmost respect throughout my years.

To all my friends for their friendship, and to all my teammates over the years and opposition alike because without them my legacy would not exist.

Camillo for his friendship and loyalty through all the years.

To Sasha for my son Daniel.

Bryon Saunders from Itec Evolve who has been a great friend and partner in the short time of our friendship.

Kevin Ferguson, CEO of Highbury, for his friendship and for believing in me and this book.

Mark Keohane, who I hated when I was a rugby player and he was reporting on the Springboks, now one of my closest friends and colleagues.

Robin Hoekstra and Gary Canning, who is fighting Motor Neuron Disease, for all their friendship and support.

Last but not least a special mention to my friend and business partner Les Vos.

AUTHOR'S NOTE

Thank you to James for holding nothing back in telling his life story.

A special thanks to the Caroline family for allowing me to turn 15 on Pratt in Arniston into a writer's hut.

A shout-out to Zelim Nel as editor and huge gratitude to my children Oliver and Julia for always being an inspiration.

CONTENTS

Unconditional love	1
Rough and tough in Jeppe	13
Out of place in Bloem	26
Oh, take me back to the old Transvaal	31
From boy to man in 1994	47
Seeing red in P.E.	60
Dawn of the pro era	65
1996 winter of content	79
Lured onto the dark side	89
Mallett: a player's coach	100
Enjoying the limelight	107
Dealing with distraction	125
Soaring with the Boks	135
Drugs, rucks and rolls	144
Taking my eye off the ball	154
'Friends' nearly ruined me	161
Thrown a rugby lifeline	170
2002: Not a great vintage	174
Straeuli a big letdown	180
Hanging up my Bok blazer	192
Betrayed by my wife	196
Living life after rugby	200
Bok career at a glance	207

UNCONDITIONAL LOVE

As we opened the car door to leave the Gecko Lounge just before 1am I heard a gunshot. What followed was the most haunting of cries: all he could muster was a pained and defeated "Aaaah!"

I swung round to see the gunmen, leaning out of a moving BMW, put more bullets into his slumped body. It all lasted no more than 10 seconds but it felt like an eternity from the moment I heard the gunshot, till getting him into the back of the car to rush him to the hospital. He didn't say anything. He couldn't say anything. I was powerless as I watched the colour drain from his face. I can't remember what I said or was saying. I just wanted him to fight, but the bullets had done all the fighting. He was dying while I was watching and by the time I carried him into the emergency operating theatre, his body was lifeless.

One of my best friends was dead. He had been assassinated.

Carlo Binne was just 26 when he died in my arms in April 2001. He was the second friend I had lost to an assassination after Julio Buscelli was killed in October, 1999.

Both were the victims of an orchestrated hit. They often spoke about the possibility of their lives ending in bloodshed. Six months before Carlo's death, he had been seriously wounded in an assassination attempt outside the Bourbon Street nightclub in Randburg.

It was the world both of my friends inhabited. It wasn't my world but I had enough insight into it to know these things could happen. I just never imagined Carlo being shot in the back within arm's reach of me.

It will forever numb me. Nothing can prepare you to hold a friend as he takes his final breaths.

It doesn't matter the day, the month or the year; it plays out in my mind, over and over. The recall, like the shooting, comes without warning and every time it is as brutal as the moment it happened. And every time I think about it all I can see is the pained and perplexed expression on Carlo's face.

I still mourn Carlo and Julio's deaths. The emotion will never subside. To me, they were good okes. They were loyal men in a brotherhood of men. They were fearless in the way they lived but they were equally gentle in what they gave to our friendship.

I wanted to tell my life story, in part to take ownership of my decisions, and also to set the record straight on the many perceptions about me that are presented as fact.

I have made many poor decisions and mistakes, and I have regrets. There are so many things I would do differently but apologising for my friendship with Carlo and Julio isn't one of them. They made their own decisions about how they lived and the path of business they chose. I never judged them for it and it never impacted on our friendship. They were a massive part of my life and they reinforced the value of friendship and the depth a connection needs for it to be called a friendship. I want to thank them publicly for the good and crazy times, and for the brotherhood. As you read on, you'll get to understand me better through the many wonderful and colourful characters that have been in my life. And hopefully you'll appreciate them as I do.

I want to share my highs and those magical moments that make it all seem worthwhile, and it is important for me to speak about the lows and the ugly moments that make us all question the world we live in and some of the people we think are friends.

I have two children, Daniel James (9) and Mila Jamie (6). They are my everything.

Their names and date of birth are tattooed on my upper inner arms so they know they will forever be a part of me. I see Mila most days and speak to her every day. She loves ice-skating and horse riding and loves telling stories. She has the most enduring imagination and she makes me laugh. I think I make her laugh as well and I know she likes to spend time with her dad. She knows how much I want to be with her and how I cherish taking her to school and fetching her. She also knows how much I care for her mom Claire.

I couldn't have asked for a more amazing mother to my daughter Mila. Claire gave me the gift of Mila but she also has given me so much more when it comes to love, understanding, acceptance and forgiveness. I can't apologise enough to her for my mistakes, when it came to the two of us. I regret so much for breaking her heart and want her to know how much I will always love her and how much it means that we will always be bonded as a family by little Mila.

Sasha-Lee is the mother of Daniel. We called him our miracle little man because of her struggles to fall pregnant. When she eventually did, thanks to our investment in fertility procedures, we were blessed with 3.3 kilograms of boy beauty.

I don't see Daniel at the moment and I have no contact with him. It is not through choice.

I want him in my life and I have always wanted him to be my boy and for him to be around his dad, but I can't get to him to tell him. Perhaps he will one day read this book and know exactly how hard I fought to be his legal guardian, custodian and dad.

I love you Daniel and I never wanted to hurt you. My absence from your life is not because I don't care about you or love you. I dream of the day you and Mila are at the ice-skating rink with me.

I will never give up hope of us all sitting at the same dining table and hearing the two of you tell me your stories. If I could have one wish come true then it would be for you, Daniel, to know your dad and your sister. It would be for you to be with us.

Daniel, your name was inspired by the Bible's Daniel. It is a strong name. Your mom and I wanted you to have a strong name because it took so much strength for you to be born. Your second name is your dad and granddad's and you carry the Dalton surname.

Be proud of who you are. Be proud of your family legacy and be proud to be a Dalton.

Your father has lived an interesting life and it is one I want to share with you. I want you and Mila to understand why certain things happened. I want you to know when I erred and also when I soared. There has never been an opportunity for me to sit with you Daniel because when your mother and I separated you were too young to have this talk.

I want you to know how much I think of you and just how it hurts not having you close.

Just the other day Mila, Claire and I were at a local restaurant in Newlands (Cape Town). There were a few boys playing with a soccer ball and they were getting a bit reckless in where they were kicking the ball. I asked them to keep it outside with the ball. One of the youngsters asked me if I was James Dalton.

I said I was and he responded: "You are Daniel's dad."

I was immediately taken aback. I had not seen Daniel in two years, and even then, the interaction was in a car park and lasted a few minutes. It would have been closer to five years when Daniel and I were last together.

"Daniel misses you," the boy said. "We google you a lot to see photos and Daniel likes to read about your rugby."

The tears welled up. I had to fight not to cry in that moment.

"Daniel used to play rugby but he doesn't anymore. He plays soccer," added the boy.

I asked why Daniel no longer played rugby and the boy said it was because the other boys mocked him for having a Springbok dad who didn't love him, didn't care about him and didn't ever come to watch him play.

My heart broke in that moment and until you are back in my life, Daniel, it will always be broken.

This is the story of you and my fight to get you.

You were born on 30 November, 2009.

Your mom and I lived in Silverlakes and we wanted to have a baby boy. You came into this world because of choice and our desire to be parents.

We wanted only the best for you and I wanted the best for your mom. I employed a night nurse and a nanny so that your mom could rest well in the evenings and be strong for you in the day. Your mom loved you and you had a great start to your life because two loving parents wanted you born into this world.

Your mom's family lived in Cape Town and we didn't see much of them in your first two years. I had a civil relationship with the family but, like most families, your mother's family had a history of conflict and there were issues between your mom and her sister and also your mom and your grandparents.

Your mom was a beauty queen when she was younger. She was a runner up for the Miss South Africa title. She took a lot of strain when she was younger and her mom put a lot of pressure on her to always be the prettiest, the most beautiful and the most elegant at these pageants. It was more the mom's dream than Sasha's to be Miss South Africa and neither recovered from her coming so close but not being crowned the queen of South Africa.

Sasha had a lot of mental health issues and also suffered because of substance abuse.

She was battling with motherhood. It wasn't the emotional side of having a child and loving him but the operational responsibilities. It overwhelmed her and her inability to cope strained our relationship.

There was a situation in 2011 when Sasha was admitted to Life Fourways Clinic. The managing director of EMER-G-MED, Wayne Grindell, issued a statement on her condition. "Sasha's emaciated state was one where she could clearly not be left alone and was of no sound judgement to take care of herself or make rational decisions. She had been living on condensed milk and cream soda and clearly needed intervention. We intervened in the best possible manner to ensure that the patient was taken care of throughout her trip to hospital. James Dalton had called, expressing his concern and requested that she be given the best possible care."

There were other incidents that made it impossible to continue to deny the seriousness of the situation and the mental deterioration of Sasha.

The solution was to send Sasha and Daniel to Cape Town, so that she could be near her parents and that Daniel could have that additional family support structure but still be close enough to see his mother. It was a decision made from the heart and with all the intent of everyone winning but it proved to be a decision that would ultimately lead to me losing my son.

It had become unbearable for Sasha and I to be together. She was bipolar and was in and out of rehabilitation. Living with a person with a personality disorder and with a substance abuse problem was so challenging, especially when I was dealing with so much personally at the time. I had been trying to finalise my divorce to Andrea who had accused me of trying to murder her during the time we were married.

Andrea and I were separated by the time I met Sasha, but she insisted on playing ugly games with me in the media and the delays in getting our divorce finalised added to the volatility.

I blame myself for giving too much to Sasha after Daniel's birth. She was treated like a princess mother because she was given all the support systems but never took on the real responsibilities most mothers experience.

Sasha had always been indulged. She always blamed others for her own decisions and she has never taken responsibility. She was in denial about her own situation and I was defensive about mine when it came to the protracted Andrea divorce proceedings.

There was also the nonsense of the attempted murder charge, which Andrea reported to the media before ever going to the police. Her accusation was a fabrication yet her refusal to co-operate with the police and courts, as the complainant, meant it took several court dates before the case was dismissed.

It was a messy time for Sasha and myself and sending her and Daniel to Cape Town seemed the right thing to do.

I knew that Sasha and I could not be in a relationship but it meant so much to me to be Daniel's dad and I knew how important it was for me to be an active father in my son's upbringing.

I provided all the financial support that was needed and for the next two years I commuted to Cape Town on weekends to spend time with Daniel. I think I missed three weekends in those two years.

On the 23rd August, 2012 I got a phone call from a social services lady by the name of Tania Nell. She informed me that Daniel was being placed with his grandparents because his mother (Sasha) was incapable of looking after him. I was told Sasha was on the verge of a complete mental breakdown and in need of urgent psychiatric care. She was unable to care for her child and was irrational and aggressive in her behaviour. Sasha had again been placed in rehabilitation for treatment.

I asked why I was never contacted as Daniel's father to go to Cape Town and be with him or to bring him to Johannesburg. After all, I was his father and was very much a part of his life. I wanted the responsibility of custody and was angered due process had not been followed.

Why the grandparents? Why not his dad?

I had been blindsided. The family had spent the two years manipulating a situation to get me out of Daniel's life.

Sasha was in a poor state and all the medical reports detailed just why she was not in a fit state to care for Daniel but none of the reports were about me. The family wanted to make it about me and they engaged Leigh Pettigrew, an educational psychologist, to make the case that I was an unfit father, and that any contact with Daniel would have to be under the supervision of a social services expert whose fee would be for my expense.

Pettigrew made damning allegations and her reports to the Child Court suggested I was a danger to Daniel because of my friendships with people she described as gangsters and because I had been considered an aggressive rugby player. She also argued that she was concerned I would not have the emotional capacity to deal with a three-year-old and that this had the potential to endanger Daniel's life.

Her reports were baseless, in terms of fact or procedure, and yet she was prepared to make recommendations based on consulting sessions with me that totalled less than seven hours.

The Health Professions Council of South Africa would later charge her with two counts of unprofessional conduct (arising between November 2012 and March 2015) in that she first failed to obtain corroborative evidence in the form of psychological assessment and later contravened an ethical rule in failing to attend consultations despite numerous requests.

Sasha, her parents and Pettigrew attacked my character and asserted that their opinion of me was reason enough to force supervised visits on me or no visits at all.

They used media reports of alleged violence during my rugby career and the media reports of Andrea's accusation to undermine me. They alleged that Daniel was unsafe in my company and I was subjected to the humiliating reality of having to visit my son with court supervision.

It was an awful situation because I had not seen it coming. Sasha was in rehabilitation, her parents would not engage with me and I found myself involved in the fight of my life just to be able to see my son.

Social workers had questioned Daniel's safety around his mother and the Children's Court in Wynberg ordered Daniel to be placed in the temporary care of Sasha's parents, pending the finalisation of the enquiry.

The battle to get custody of my son had started and it would take me to hell and back because I agreed to comply with whatever requirement, however unjust, to prove I was a loving father who was capable and committed to caring for his son.

I went for a full psychiatric assessment, for liver diagnosis in relation to accusations of alcohol abuse, for random drug tests and I agreed to pay for two specialists to supervise my visits with Daniel, which totalled nearly 200 hours. I also agreed to assessments with clinical psychologist Terence Dowdall.

I had made my mistakes as a youth, lost the plot socially in the late 1990s and early 2000s and never disputed that there was a time in my life when boozing and the use of recreational drugs temporarily derailed my rugby career and search for happiness.

But I fought those demons to make an international comeback for the Springboks in 2002 and I had fought those demons to become a father. I took my responsibility of fatherhood seriously, otherwise I would not have exposed myself to the emotional risk that comes with fertility procedures.

I wanted to be judged on fact and not my past, or a perception of my past. What had I done since Daniel's birth that would ruled me a danger to him? I had never been assessed as a potential caregiving parent but the recommendation from Pettigrew was based on what she had heard from Daniel's grandparents. It was a set-up because the grandparents wanted me out of Daniel's life and they wanted Daniel. They knew Sasha would always be unsuitable for sole custody because of her addiction issues but if I was still in Daniel's life as the primary caregiver they risked losing Daniel at a time when they must have felt like they were losing their daughter.

They made accusations that I had physically abused Sasha but there was no evidence to support it and no case had ever been reported to the police because it had ever happened. We had argued often – and verbally abused each other – but there was no physical violence or attacks.

There is never an excuse for verbal abuse and I was conscious of the effects on a young child who hears their parents arguing. I grew up in a household where both my parents gave me love but they didn't always give each other the same kind of love. I knew how it affected me as a child and how I hated hearing them screaming, arguing and insulting each other.

Why would I put Daniel through that? I challenged Pettigrew's assertions, allegations, accusations and skewed assessment, conclusions and recommendations.

Dowdall, the clinical psychologist, interviewed both supervision specialists, who spent nearly 200 hours observing my visits with Daniel. In his report he stated it was unprecedented to have two mental health professionals with this level of experience observing a parent over several months for 200 hours. He expressed his confidence in their observations and conclusions.

Raella Abel had spent 78 hours with Daniel and myself and Anne Cawood 120 hours.

Both commented on the warm and loving relationship that exists between father and son.

Anne, in her report, stated: "His relationship with the child is brilliant. Not once has Danny not wanted to come – he rushes up to James, hugs him, then says, 'Where's Danny going today?' When he hadn't seen his dad for two weeks, he was rubbing his father's head saying, 'I miss you, my dad. I love you, my dad'. I see an exceptionally close and warm bond."

Pettigrew's main area of concern was how I would respond to Daniel's potential anger in a situation? She asserted that I was someone who was not connected with my own anger issues and that I could quite easily react aggressively back to a child of that age who was "throwing a temper tantrum with a great deal of primitive and unprocessed anger".

This was also answered in all my assessments because there were occasions Daniel had a temper tantrum during our supervised visits. I calmly dealt with it and both experts reported on these outcomes.

I had put myself through 200 hours of supervised visits with my son and no visit was allowed unless I paid in advance for the right to see my son in the presence of appointed social worker experts.

I had volunteered to the humiliation of every test and examination to prove I was not unstable and unsuitable to care for my child.

Both Raella and Anne, in their reports, concluded I posed no risk to Daniel and that there was no further justification for supervised contact.

Dowdall, in his summary and recommendations, mentioned the heightened conflicts caused because of Sasha's drug abuse and he also divorced my relationship with Daniel, as his father, to the breakdown of my relationship with Sasha, as my partner.

Dowdall described me as a "stimulating, affirming parent, who is fully engaged with his child and deals emphatically and positively with him. James is a good, committed and loving father. I do not believe supervision is warranted and agree fully with Ms Abel and Ms Cawood in this regard."

The reports all concurred that the allegations about me not being a father fit enough to look after my son were absurd and yet there would be no respite nor resolution. The grandparents were unrelenting and after two bitter years of me doing everything to be with my son, they waited until the 29th December, 2014 to serve High Court papers notifying me that they would be contesting for full custody of Daniel.

I was finished, mentally drained and exhausted. The financial cost had been extreme, in excess of R2million, and they had waited to the end of the year to drop this last bomb on me.

I just couldn't continue. They had taken away my integrity and my self-respect. They had forced me to submit to the most demeaning tests. They had insulted my character and paraded perception as fact.

They had taken away my rights to do anything for my son. They had denied Daniel a relationship with his little sister and they consciously promoted the propaganda that I wasn't capable of caring for my son.

I was done. I was defeated.

Mila's mom Claire knew the grandparents because she and Sasha had been friends who had drifted in and out of each other's lives. Claire reached out to the grandfather recently for Daniel and Mila to spend time with each other. He refused to respond.

I couldn't believe that after four years there was still such animosity from his side. The grandmother has since passed and Sasha continues to have problems with addiction. I know that Claire and Mila would offer Daniel such a positive reinforcement.

What kind of monster denies a boy the right to a loving father?

Daniel saw me in the parking lot of a mall in Tokai two years ago. He was in the car and he was with his mother. He put his head into his hands and started to cry. I walked to him and hugged him hello through the car window.

His mother said: "This is your boy. Look how big he is."

I couldn't contain my emotions and I burst into tears. Daniel was crying and I was crying. Sasha wasn't. She just stared at both of us.

I told him: "I'll always be your dad and I will always love you."

ROUGH AND TOUGH IN JEPPE

Jeppe High School for Boys' biggest rival is King Edward VII School (KES). My matric year coincided with Jeppe's centenary in 1990, and the highlight of the season was hosting KES in what is the school's most famed derby.

A week before the KES showdown we were due to play Athlone Boys High from Johannesburg's southern suburb of Bezuidenhout Valley, which we knew as Bez Valley.

Anyone who knows anything about Johannesburg's southern suburbs knows that sophistication comes in the form of physical strength. Rightly or wrongly, reputations among teenagers and young men from this area are made with fists and not necessarily intellect. If you had both, you were a jewel and most definitely a diamond in the rough.

I'd like to think of myself as the latter. Those who know me will be laughing with me right at this moment - contrary to media reports, I do have a sense of humour and am capable of laughing at myself as much as I laugh at the next person.

We had a decent side at Jeppe in 1990 and I had a big reputation as a schoolboy rugby player with pedigree and the potential to become a Springbok. I was in my second year playing for the First XV and later made the (old Transvaal and now Lions) provincial schools team at Craven Week and the South African Schools team.

I was also well-known for working at one of the popular nightclubs in Johannesburg, even though I was only 16 years old. I had a street reputation as a teenager; some of it was justified but most of it was based on urban legend. I came from a very strict household, being the only son of a disciplinarian father who was a policeman and spent his entire working life in the South African Police Force.

My sport was important to me during high school, and sport for me extended beyond rugby. I played everything and I was most seduced by strength training in the gym, long before it was fashionable for schoolboy sporting hopefuls to make gym part of their daily routine.

My father was my inspiration, which doesn't mean he was, or is, without fault. As a family, we lived off a policeman's salary and in a police house in Cumberland Road in Kensington. It was a small house with a metal fence, metal gates and a tin roof.

I am embarrassed to say it now but there was a time when I was younger that I was ashamed of my modest upbringing. I would see the wealth that others had - the houses they stayed in and the cars they came to school in - and I would feel inferior. Perhaps this was the reason I put so much emphasis on my sport and being successful on the rugby field, where I could feel like I was the one to be envied for my talent.

Despite my insecurities about our lack of wealth, I never felt that I wanted for anything. My father was always there to offer support and to make me believe that anything was possible. When I was in primary school, he transported me to wherever I needed to be. If I wanted to do karate, he created the opportunity. If it was wrestling or judo, cricket or soccer, it didn't matter. I got to train with South African judo icon Dougie Baggott and his many impressive sons. I also got to watch *Pippie Langkous* on television as a six-year-old, and I have no problem admitting that it was my favourite show back then.

My dad was always strong in allowing me to try everything and was instrumental in me supplementing my rugby in the early part of my career with training at Nicky Ness' Amateur Boxing Club in Booysens. I'd go from rugby training to doing 10 rounds of pads with Nicky, who was among the most passionate people I had met and the greatest of amateur boxing trainers.

I loved primary school and never missed a day in seven years as a youngster at Kensington Primary, which is now Eastgate Primary.

There was so much to do at school every day and so many different sports to play. My dad provided the best for me at all times. Cricket and soccer were my games when I was younger and if I could give my dad a rand for every throw down or ball bowled to me, he'd be bloody rich today. He even built a cricket net for me in our backyard.

He wasn't a vocal dad and he never got intense or involved. He would watch my rugby matches from 30-40 metres away. He wasn't the type of father to stand next to the field and scream instructions but when he did speak afterwards, I'd listen. He observed but never objected. I would want to know his opinion and what he felt of the match or my performance but I never felt the pressures I've seen in so many players and their fathers. He was a supporter in how he loved and cared for me but he also enjoyed just spending time with me, and I certainly wanted to have him around and spend time with him.

My father had a fractured relationship with his father, who was a drunk and had abandoned the family when my dad was young. My grandfather wasn't in his life but he also wasn't exactly out of it because my dad has told me of the many times he would find his granddad passed out and drunk on the streets near Jeppe, or hear him hurling abuse from outside the Jeppe Police Station.

My grandfather's abuse of alcohol also explains why my father doesn't drink alcohol and the way in which my father loves me would be in contrast to the absence of love he got from his father. Sadly, my grandfather drank himself to death and he died a lonely man.

My father has always been a constant in my life and although I went to English-speaking schools, I have always spoken Afrikaans to him. The thing I am so blessed about is that for all the support I got from my dad, he did it without ever wanting to live a different life through me. Whatever I did was about me and not about him. He was strict in what he expected from me as a person and if my father instilled one thing in me, it was discipline.

If I wanted to be the best then I had to train and I had to train on the days when my opponent would be resting. I'd run from my home to the gym and be inspired by the run back home after each session. I mingled with an older crowd who were powerlifters and weightlifters. I dreamed of being Mr Universe and going to the United States to claim glory on the grandest of stages. The teenage me aspired to a bodybuilding future more than any provincial and international rugby career. And through boxing I got confidence in my physical ability and realised that aerobic and cardiovascular conditioning were as important as muscle mass.

I took pride in the way I trained and applied myself to being stronger, fitter and more confident than my opponent, and all my mates will tell you that it didn't matter if we had a bender Saturday night, I'd be up at 5am, hungover or not, on my way to Jeppe to run the hills and the 2.4-kilometre time trial.

I knew that working to be the best comes with sacrifice. I was taught to respect my opponent but never fear him. Toughness was as much about the mind as the body, but a fit body makes for a fitter mind. It is easier to push the mind when the mind knows the body is conditioned.

I wasn't captain of Jeppe but I was very much the guy my teammates looked to as an on-field leader, one who never took a backwards step and was always at their side when needed. I'd like to think I played a bigger game then I ever had to talk, and that brings me back to the bums from Bez Valley, whose players were hyping the match as the one in which they would take me down and show everyone who the real tough guys were in the south.

There was one particular player who may have been big in Bez Valley but we had never heard of him in Jeppe. He put the word out that he was coming for me, to teach me a lesson in the match.

I had become used to that sort of showboating when working the door at the nightclub. I'd often get threats from guys who I wouldn't let into to the club because they were underage. They all had a lot to say after they'd turned their backs and walked away but weren't as talkative when they were within arm's reach.

Initially, I didn't think much of the talk coming out of Bez Valley. But each day I'd be told another story about this supposed bruiser who was going to thump me. I'd never met this guy but he was sending messages that he wasn't scared of me or the 'Dalton factor' and that he was going to give me a physical beating.

We were told the agitation and aggression was coming from a guy who was their flanker and supposed enforcer. Jake White, who would coach the Springboks to the 2007 World Cup, was the Jeppe First XV coach, and Jake's Jeppe teams, like all the teams he has coached professionally, thrived on physical intensity.

Jake encouraged aggression and, especially among schoolboys, knew how matches could be won through the sheer force of a physical approach.

But, as I would experience throughout my professional rugby career, there is a difference between being physical and being a thug. There were teams I played against (when at Transvaal and with the Springboks) that were renowned for being direct and abrasive, in the rugby sense.

You'd leave the field battered, and it was because of how it felt to tackle them and how they tackled you. The aches and pains were a result of them hurting us in the scrums or at the breakdown. These teams, who earned my respect, did so because of rugby and not because they were off-the-ball cowards.

There is nothing to respect or revere about someone who blindsides you with a punch or who strikes when your hands are bound under a ruck, and there is nothing tough about anyone who uses a rugby field as a platform for fighting.

I had never highly rated a team from Athlone Boys' for their rugby ability and had never been intimidated by their physicality because I believed we were a good enough rugby team to be successful against them. There was also enough fight and mongrel among our players to stand up to their cheap shots.

Jake made sure we knew what to expect in this match and he also made sure there would be an on-field consequence to us standing back in any confrontation. If they hit us off the ball and there was no counter, they would interpret it as a sign of weakness and they would get confidence from it because it would allow them to slow down the game and disrupt our fluency. We were a team that played with physical intent but we also played with pace. We considered ourselves a good rugby side. We weren't running out to prove a point after their endless trash-talking in the build-up but it was clear to us that if the moment of confrontation arrived, we had to make a point.

Jake had told us to focus on our rugby, beat them with skill and the rest would look after itself. Equally, Jake was a coach who would take it personally if his teams got roughed up or physically took a bashing. We were prepared for the worst.

Typically, they offered nothing in the match, and all the pre-match bark had no bite. The Bez Valley flanker who was going to give me a beating didn't utter a word. When it came to the rucks he was on the wing and at scrum time he was last to engage and first to detach. There was a time in the match when I thought he had left the field because he was nowhere to be seen.

We controlled the game and were playing good rugby. There had been no incidents and, physically, they were no match for us. There wasn't much time left, maybe 10 minutes, when they finally struck in the most cowardly fashion. Our tighthead prop Brent Moyle, who would play for the Springboks in the early 2000s, was pumped in an off-the-ball incident.

Brent had been tackled near the touchline, play moved on and then, as Brent got up to return to play, he was punched by the flanker who had done all the pre-match trash-talking.

It was the cheapest of shots because Brent was unaware of what was coming, was not in a position to defend himself and, on impact from the strike, fell like a sack of potatoes being dropped from the third storey. He was knocked out and wasn't moving. As he hit the ground, more Athlone players moved in on Brent to continue the assault. This was the moment they'd been waiting for all match, when a second-rate team turns a rugby match into a street fight.

I got to Brent first and stood over him to protect them kicking him, and in looking up I got sight of this flanker who had done the dirty on Brent. He was charging in on me. In that moment it was game on and before he could even lift his fist, I smoked him and fractured his cheekbone. I broke that cheekbone proper. That punch of mine sparked a free-for-all and it was full-on between the two teams.

I didn't see that flanker again. I never heard from him or of him and I reckon he must have moved out of Bez Valley. Parents, teachers and the Jeppe and Athlone headmasters rushed onto the field to stop the fighting and separate the teams. The referee, on the instruction of Jeppe's headmaster, ended the match prematurely.

Jeppe's headmaster, Mr Quail wasn't ever going to be on my Christmas list. I didn't enjoy him as a principal or as a person and the feeling was mutual. I knew I was in trouble afterwards when Quail came storming into our change room to tell us how disgusted he was with our behaviour and, in particular, mine.

Jake didn't challenge the headmaster. As Quail screamed, Jake cowered and the headmaster left having told the team there would be a follow-up and disciplinary on the Monday morning, and when I got to school, I was duly summoned to the headmaster's office. I knew I wasn't about to be applauded for defending a helpless teammate.

There was no love lost in the meeting. Quail did all the talking and he was adamant about making an example of me, handing down a suspension that ruled me out of the Centenary match against KES, and temporarily stripping me of my Full Colours blazer. He said I had embarrassed the school and now he was going to embarrass me.

Jeppe is the oldest known school in Johannesburg and one of the oldest in South Africa. It is steeped in history and, with more than 100 years of tradition, it's an educational institution that has produced many famous names in politics, literature, business and sport, with a handful of cricketers playing for South Africa and two Springboks in Des Sinclair and Wilf Rosenberg.

I would become Jeppe's first professional Springbok rugby player but in that meeting in the headmaster's office, Quail wasn't looking at me thinking 'future Springbok'. His expression screamed expulsion but he also knew that there were no grounds for such drastic action.

I never stayed in the Jeppe High catchment area, so geographically I wasn't automatically eligible for enrolment in Grade 8. My dad's standing, as a police officer who worked most of his career at Jeppe, influenced me getting into Jeppe, and I was well aware that this meant I owed it to my father, as much as the traditions of Jeppe, to always give of my best in high school. I wasn't academically in the top set and was more of a C than an A-aggregate student, but I was diligent with my school work, excelled on the sports field and endorsed, promoted and echoed Jeppe's values.

My dad never interfered, even though I know it could have changed the headmaster's attitude had he been present on that Monday morning. In the aftermath of the match, my father was of the view that Jake, as my coach, and myself were equipped to deal with any disciplinary against me.

That was fine with me because I didn't want my dad fighting my battles. I was a leader among the schoolboys and I felt the headmaster could have shown greater understanding of the situation and of my reaction to what was going to happen after Brent got knocked out.

Many years later, in an article written by Clinton van der Berg in the South African Sunday Times, Jake spoke about the Jeppe incident. Clinton quoted Jake as saying that 10 school masters had called him to arrange a one-off friendly in the week, so that I would serve my one-match suspension and still be available for the KES Centenary match.

The article quotes Jake as saying: "Naturally, I was tempted, as KES had a very good team, and my side, while good relied heavily on (James) Dalton. But the headmaster wouldn't agree."

Jake, in the Monday morning meeting, was very silent and I didn't know until then quite how disgusted I would be with Jake as my First XV coach. I'd always given everything for my teammates and for Jake as the coach. I put Jeppe first but Jake clearly put himself first. I needed my coach to stand tall for me but he was dwarfed in the presence of the headmaster and when I needed Jake to have a voice, he looked at me, lost in voice, unwilling to say anything. It was as if he had a bad case of bronchitis.

Jeppe's motto is the Latin, *Forti nihil difficilius* which in English translates to "For the brave, nothing is too difficult."

I didn't think of Jake in that meeting as being brave or of

showing me that nothing is too difficult. All I saw was a self-serving mute. I really expected more from Jake, who was among a rare breed to have attended and taught at Jeppe. I knew what Jeppe meant to Jake and he knew what the school meant to me, and how I would give everything for the team's cause.

He was always happy for me to play the role of the enforcer and to give his team momentum and he was always comfortable for me to lead from the front. Now I needed him to lead as the coach and to back me. He just didn't and it is something I will never forget because he was someone with the gift of the gab who never had a problem talking. Yet the one time I needed him to talk, he had lost his voice.

That day I lost all respect for him as a man, even though I continued to support him as a coach and give my best in every training session and match for the rest of the season.

Jake, in my view, is a coach who was very good with schoolboys and with younger players because he could dominate them and be dictatorial and not have his ways challenged. It is why he has struggled and clashed with so many senior players in settled professional teams. It is very different getting into the head of a youngster than it is a hardened and experienced veteran. As schoolboy players, Jake would talk all of us up. He would whip us into a frenzy with some great speeches and he would make everyone believe they were a lot better than was necessarily the case. He could bullshit and we all bought his bullshit because it played into young egos.

I didn't find him a particularly inspiring coach tactically or technically. He wasn't innovative and relied on fitness, conditioning, discipline and physicality. Like all successful schoolboy rugby coaches, he got us fit, and if you tell a schoolboy rugby player to run all day, he will.

Jake's strength in schoolboy rugby was his simplicity in sticking to those basic principles and it has worked for him professionally where he had success with the Springboks, Brumbies, Sharks and Montpellier. He coached the Springboks to the 2007 World Cup title and that was a brilliant achievement, but when I hear how few of that squad talk to him and how all the teams he did well with were happy for him to leave, it reinforced what I experienced from him as a person in the headmaster's office on that Monday morning.

Jake had the vision to move me from flanker to hooker in my final two years at Jeppe, and for that I will always be grateful. He saw the potential in me as a future Springbok hooker and told me that while he thought I was a good loose forward, I could become one of the world's best as a hooker. I trusted his rugby brain and I worked hard to prove that he hadn't got it wrong in investing in me as a hooker, but if Jake had qualities as a rugby coach, I didn't feel the same about him as a man. I just never trusted him and when he stood in absolute silence in the headmaster's office, it only affirmed why I didn't trust him.

He was known as Jake the Snake because he would have your back if it benefitted his cause, but if there was no gain in it for Jake, you'd find yourself standing alone. Jake was spineless. He was a schoolboy coach who lived through his players. He is someone who takes more than he gives and wherever he goes he burns bridges and rubbishes people.

Jake and Kitch Christie are both World Cup-winning Springbok coaches who I played under. The only thing they have in common is a World Cup trophy because there's no comparison between them as rugby coaches or people.

Quail suspended me on the Monday morning and by first break the entire school knew of the headmaster's action.

The schoolboys, who numbered close to 1000, refused to accept my suspension. They all felt I had honoured the ethos of the school by defending a teammate. I had stood over an unconscious Brent Moyle and they were determined to stand over me.

I was flattered and, more than it boosting my ego, it humbled me. My coach couldn't do it but boys, regardless of their grade or their association with me, wanted to defend me.

The headmaster demanded the boys return to their classrooms, but they wouldn't. A staff meeting followed and then a special assembly in which the headmaster attempted to explain why he was compelled to suspend me. The boys still refused to go back to class unless my suspension was lifted and I was available to play against KES. Quail pleaded with them and when this didn't work, he asked them to consider what he had said and to let him know their feelings by 8am on the Tuesday.

Jeppe's schoolboys, on that Monday, were on strike and the news spread throughout the community. Representatives of the Transvaal Education Department were called to the school and the story was on the front pages of the provincial newspapers the next day.

The headmaster, in the course of the afternoon, had also spoken to players in the First XV, but he had not done so as a collective. He separated the matrics from the grade 11s, knowing that the matrics wouldn't and couldn't be bullied. He could still intimidate those who were going to be in school the following year. He divided the First XV to get the outcome that he wanted, which was that they agreed to play the Centenary match against KES despite my suspension.

Once he got some of the boys to agree to get on with it without me, the rest of the team eventually agreed. I never held it against the team because I never expected them to boycott the match. The team was bigger than me and Jeppe, as an institution, was not about one player in a rugby team.

Obviously, I wanted to be playing in the Centenary match because it was a one-off that was a first and a last and there will never be another Jeppe Centenary match against KES.

The team had agreed to play KES but the rest of the school was still on strike. They would only stop if the suspension stopped.

Quail called me to his office and asked me to put the school first, which I had only ever done. He implored me to convince the boys to return to class, and I told him that I would do it and that I would also be back to get my Full Colours' blazer, something I did a week later.

Quail called another assembly for me to speak to the boys. I was overwhelmed with what the entire school had done, but I also knew they would be putting themselves at a disadvantage if they continued to strike.

I agreed to ask the boys to go back to class but then Quail also wanted me to read an apology he had prepared on my behalf. I refused and said I would write my own speech, which he then wanted to edit before I spoke.

I again refused and asked him if he wanted me to convince the boys to go back to class or not?

I never wrote a speech or read out any prepared headmaster's apology speech, but I spoke from the heart and told the boys what they did in solidarity for me as one of their own spoke to Jeppe's motto of being brave and showing that nothing was too difficult.

I asked them to go back to class and they did.

Jeppe hosted KES in the Centenary match that Saturday without me and lost, but I did get to play in the return match later in the season, and we won.

OUT OF PLACE IN BLOEM

The reward for my rugby at Jeppe was a scholarship to the University of the Free State (UFS), but the reality was that the move from Johannesburg to Bloemfontein was to play rugby more than it was to study. I can't tell you the course I signed up for because I can't recall getting to many classes…

It was all about the rugby, to be part of the Varsity Under-20 side and to hopefully impress enough to make the Free State U20s and the SA Universities U20s in 1991.

The rugby was a step up from everything I'd experienced at Jeppe. The quality of player was in another league and the rugby recruitment by UFS meant many players had been drafted from around the country. I'd never trained with so many good players, who were all trying to make the same team.

Culturally, being in Bloemfontein was a shock for me. The City of Roses is another world when compared to Johannesburg. Afrikaans is my father's first language while my mother is English-speaking. I was schooled in English at Jeppe and that was the language I was most accustomed to but in Bloemfontein they spoke English only out of extreme necessity. When I did get to lectures, I found it near impossible to cope with Afrikaans lectures and studying from Afrikaans textbooks.

I was in Bloemfontein thanks to the influence of former Springbok fullback Gysie Pienaar, who knew my father and had been sufficiently impressed with what he had seen of me as a schoolboy.

Brendan Venter, who would be my Rugby World Cup teammate in 1995, was my residence father and back then it was more Mr Venter than Brendan. The Afrikaans-speaking culture was like nothing I had known and I struggled. It was a foreign environment and I battled to understand, let alone appreciate, the nuances of the culture in the context of hierarchy and archaic-type disciplines.

Socially, it was also an adaptation that I never quite mastered and this big-city boy never found solace in a town with very few lights.

The rugby field was about the only place I felt at home and I was fortunate to experience the coaching of Oom Tat Botha. A popular question to every retired Springbok player is who were the best coaches they played under, and Oom Tat is definitely in my top three.

Obviously, my Transvaal and World Cup-winning Springbok coach Kitch Christie stands head and shoulders above the rest, and for those of you familiar with boxing, you'll get it when I say he was to me what Cus D'Amato was to Mike Tyson. Kitch was as much mentor, father and disciplinarian, as he was rugby coach.

Jake White, who later led the Springboks to glory at the 2007 Rugby World Cup, was my Jeppe coach during my final two years at school. He was the only measurement I had when getting to Bloemfontein and Oom Tat and Jake were polar opposites.

Jake saw Jeppe as a stepping stone to the next level of coaching - he always aspired to the Springbok job and he was willing to do anything to get there. Oom Tat was passionate about making good, young rugby players even better, and he was as interested in the person as he was in the player. Where Oom Tat lived for his players, Jake lived through his players.

Oom Tat was gentle and kind but his presence commanded

respect from all the senior and U20 players. He was held in incredibly high regard because he had improved so many young players in a short space of time and prepared them for senior rugby. He had a lovely way of working with younger players and was motivated by making the player a better human being. There was more to Oom Tat than just winning rugby matches. Some coaches rule by fear, but not Oom Tat.

He was tactically very good and technically outstanding. I felt he improved a lot in my game, but always gave me enough to think about when it came to my growth as a person.

I trusted Oom Tat and felt there was honesty and transparency in our interactions. He was not driven by personal gain or ambition. It was only about the players and Oom Tat, unlike Jake, always had my back.

The Varsity U20s played in a senior league against Second XVs and we had to rely on natural talent, skill and the insights and tactical approach of Oom Tat to get our wins. The rugby was hard against older men, some who were well into their 30s, and you knew you were a boy playing against men. Their beards were darker than ours, their feet were bigger and they were physically stronger. There was no place to hide and you either had to harden the fuck up, or be fucked up.

The U20 side I played in was very talented. There were many local boys from the rugby nursery of Grey College and a lot of the boys would go on to play provincial and international rugby. Among my teammates was Naka Drotske, who in future years would be my main rival for the Springboks starting hooker position.

Naka played flank in those U20 days and I was the starting hooker. It was about the only season we really talked because I had a policy of not engaging with my rival hooker. I'm not talking about the opposition but the guy in my own squad who was competing for my position.

It is very different now because match day is about the contribution of 23 players, with rolling substitutes and, in the case of the two hookers in the squad, both have very defined roles. Both know they will get on the field, be it for the first 50 or last 30.

But when I first played U20 and senior rugby, if you didn't start the only guarantee was that your backside would suffer from those bench splinters.

I rated Naka more as a flank than a hooker and it would irritate him in future years when I would tell him at Springbok training that he should have stayed at flank because he wasn't getting the Springbok number two jersey while I was playing. It would be accurate to say that there weren't too many pleasantries between the two of us when we played for the Springboks, which suited me because I didn't relate to him as a mate.

The rugby was tough in Bloemfontein because of the physicality of those older players but it was educational because of the pedigree of my teammates and Oom Tat's coaching.

I was a better player for going to Bloemfontein and I got to know how to drink Black Label quarts but as a person, I just couldn't settle. I was out of my comfort zone, missed my mates and missed speaking English.

Living in a boarding house wasn't for me and I just couldn't go with the Afrikaans mentality that naturally leant towards some form of humiliation or physical confrontation.

I often found myself on telephone duty and the rule was never to answer a call in English. It had to be in Afrikaans and my natural inclination was to speak English. I did it one time too many and was called to task.

My punishment would be a beating with the heaviest of army boots. The drill was for the offender to hold onto a desk with both hands in a bent over position with his backside exposed to the world and the boot felt like a sledgehammer as it connected.

It was one blow too many. I'd had enough and I swung around and challenged the situation and the senior who had beaten my backside. His name was Mielie and he was unique in that he was as bright as he was big. He had brains and brawn and his hands were the same size as the size-12 boot he had been swinging at me.

I cautioned him to never again do that to me. His response was to ask me what I was going to do about it if he did. He towered over me and he had an army of seniors behind him. I learned in that moment, in that residence, that there is a time to pick your fights. If I was going to win the war of survival in Bloemfontein, then I'd have to give Mielie his victory.

This wasn't for me. The rugby may have been good, but life in Bloemfontein wasn't. I was on my way back to Johannesburg.

OH, TAKE ME BACK TO THE OLD TRANSVAAL

The year was 1992 and I was back in my version of social heaven, reunited with Camillo Zavattoni, who today remains my longest and most endearing friend.

Camillo was the Jeppe First XV tighthead prop in his matric year. Despite only being in Grade 11, I played alongside him at hooker and it was through playing together that we formed a friendship that continued to grow the following year despite him finishing school before me.

You won't find a more colourful character than Camillo and we've walked into the darkest of alleys together, experienced the wildest of times, mourned the deaths of special people and shared the most blissful moments as friends.

We've had two fallouts in 30 years and in those brief months that we didn't talk he still showed me his loyalty, refusing the offer to have me taken out because of the momentary breakdown in our friendship.

Lior Saadt, the Israeli gangster, worked as a debt collector with Camillo at that time and would later be charged with the murders of diamond dealer Shai Avissar and his estranged wife Hazel Crane. Saadt wanted to reinforce his friendship with Camillo by putting a hit on my life. When Camillo and I eventually put our differences aside, he let me know about the offer and gave me the assurance that he thought it was ridiculous.

Camillo has a great sense of humour and the way he relayed the chat between himself and Lior made me laugh. "I don't like him at the moment and I am angry with him," Camillo told Saadt. "But I still fucking want him around!"

If you don't know that world, you won't get it. Lives can be ended for what may seem very insignificant to others. Lives are taken so easily because, for the perpetrator, the act of taking out a third party strengthens the bond and loyalty between two people.

Camillo, despite his friendship and debt-collecting working relationship with Saadt, didn't need him to remove me permanently from the picture to know the two of them had each other's back every day and night that they went to work. I'll always be thankful that Camillo didn't give Lior the go-ahead. Not only did you teach me the only Italian I know, you were also kind enough to allow me to get on with my rugby career instead of worrying about what was lurking round the corner.

When I reflect on 1992, it was a year of calm and chaos. Bloemfontein was a fading memory and I was back in a familiar environment where I felt like royalty and was offered sanity, security and some extra income outside of the little there was to be made from playing rugby.

Camillo and a few other mates had introduced me to Little Holland, a brothel in Rivonia, to work the door. When I was in high school, I worked the door for a guy who owned King's Casino - I'd be there on a Wednesday night and he paid me R200. For me, it was boatloads of money and it was there that I met "Eddie the Dutchman", who was one of the most sought-after professionals in private casinos. We got along from the outset and I really enjoyed him.

Soon after I started door duty at Little Holland, Eddie opened a casino opposite Little Holland. He asked whether I would also work the door at his new casino, which meant I would double my weekly income.

I was 21 years old, playing rugby for Rand Afrikaans University (RAU) on a scholarship, the Transvaal U21s and already starting to be integrated into a bigger training squad for the senior RAU team that was coached by Oom Koos Ehlers and captained by Francois Pienaar.

My rugby was rocking but so was my social life. I didn't have a girlfriend and my loyalty was to my mates, my rugby and my part-time door duties at Little Holland and Eddie's casino. My life was rugby, gambling, alcohol and sex – it felt like I was living the dream of every 21-year-old South African male.

People are quick to label, condemn and judge without having insight into other people's lives, but as a young man working at Little Holland, I got to know so many of the women who worked the brothel and many a night was spent talking to them and listening to their stories.

There were so many shared stories of sexual abuse and hardship and even more of single moms not having other work choices because of the need to financially support a child or children. I had occasional fun, which my mates would describe as one of the perks of the job, but mostly the time spent at Little Holland was an introduction to broken spirits, souls and particularly sad eyes. My job was to provide these women with protection and not pleasure.

I was very particular as to how the men visiting Little Holland should treat the women and I made that known on entry. I accepted the place was about reward for a transaction but it didn't mean it had to be done in a demeaning way or without respect. It helped that most of the men who frequented the place were married, so they were on their best behaviour. They didn't want a scene because that would involve a beating, the potential of the police being called and then the wife being summoned to come collect them from a brothel.

Across the road at the casino, I opened the door for a different kind of animal. Money is an evil and it gives people a delusional sense of status and security. Men would arrive with attitude and arrogance because of their cheque books but they'd quickly be reminded that if they wanted to play in this world, they'd have to play to the rules.

I have always had a foot in the two contrasting worlds, that of a professional rugby player and a darker, more dangerous nightclub environment life. I chose my friends because of a connection and what the friendships meant to me. I didn't discriminate because of the professions they had chosen or the world they primarily operated in. Some were involved in the nightclub scene, others dabbled in the darker arts and were well known personalities in SA's notorious underworld with the odd cousin of mine among them. Others had links to factions and then there were my friendships with the Hells Angels in the late 1990s, in particular with Peter Conway and Rob Reynolds, who were as famous as they were infamous on the Johannesburg nightclub scene. Both are dead today.

Then there's Julio Bascelli and Carlo Binne, who I met through Camillo in the early 1990s. They were enforcers, debt collectors and did a lot of work for the Hells Angels and many others. Whatever their business choices, Julio and Carlo were among my closest friends, loyal to me as I was loyal to them, and two men who lived by the sword and eventually died by it. Both were assassinated within 18 months of Avissar's murder because they had damning evidence in relation to the hit.

Though my friendships in the early 1990s connected me to this world, it was rugby that kept me close to the straight and narrow. Having said that, it was through rugby that I met underworld kingpin Cyril Beeka in 1992.

The Transvaal U21s played Boland in Wellington that year but the squad was based in Stellenbosch. On the Saturday night, the boys wanted the brighter lights of Cape Town, so

I appointed myself designated driver and an hour later we were in the city centre.

I can't recall the place, but the boys were on the charge. They'd played a match in Wellington that afternoon and would be back in the classroom in Johannesburg on Monday morning - they were letting their hair down and being raucous. The security approached me and asked who was in charge of the players. I said I was and I was led to a guy sitting in a corner. I estimated him to be about 10 years my senior, but he was very chilled towards me. He asked me my name and wanted to know who we were.

I introduced myself as James Dalton and as the designated driver to the Transvaal U21 team.

"Ah, Jimmy," he said before standing up and introducing himself as Cyril. He asked me to keep the boys in check and guaranteed me they'd have a safe night if they understood the etiquette of the place and accepted there were patrons who also wanted to enjoy themselves. We spoke a bit about Johannesburg, the club scene and rugby. We had an immediate connection and would remain friends until his death by assassination in April 2011.

A week before his death, Cyril and I met about a possible business opportunity in which we could assist the police with the search for fugitives. In all the years I had known him, it was to be our first business venture together.

Cyril's name was synonymous with the Cape Town underworld and I was a Springbok rugby player. The media felt the two personalities should never interact, let alone be friends. I'd introduced many Springbok rugby players to Cyril over the years and Percy Montgomery also struck up a friendship with him, which is why we both attended Cyril's funeral.

The media reports lashed the two of us for being public in our support for Cyril but there was no other way to show respect to a man who we considered a friend.

I was labelled a gangster by extension and even accused of being a part of a gang, but my interactions with Cyril had never previously been about business - I never judged his profession or played in his space and he certainly didn't judge my rugby performances when I played for Transvaal or South Africa.

Cyril and I had a vibe from that first night I met him. He is the only person ever to address me as "Jimmy" on introduction. I don't do abbreviations of my name, it's a strong name and the one I was given at birth, but for some reason I didn't take offence when I first met Cyril. For the record, it never happened again - he appreciated that if I introduced myself as James then that is how I wanted to be addressed.

My high school friendships were never hidden because they didn't have to be, just as it was no secret that my dad was a respected policeman with 37 years of service, and in 1992 my friendships were strong and my rugby was getting stronger.

During the final two years at school my social life never took preference over my rugby or training. I was well conditioned and put in as many hours at the gym as I did on the field.

There have been numerous stories of steroid use in those early days and, because of my training with older body builders who had access to the drugs, it was often assumed that I was also on them. The truth is that I simply didn't have the money for steroids, but I did have the time to train to get my body stronger. My diet was one of carbs and protein and more carbs and protein.

The steroids stories were as much urban legend as the story that in a moment of rebellion I hung my First XV jersey on top of the bell tower at Jeppe. Neither happened.

What was happening was my rugby. I was making the right impression on the field at RAU, a year after leaving Bloemfontein. The studying wasn't going quite so well and this time I couldn't blame it on Bloemfontein's Afrikaans text books and lectures, I just never got to class.

In reality I was at RAU to play rugby so that I could make the Transvaal team and become a provincial player.

Up until 1992, my generation had hardly seen a Springbok team play, so it was only later that year, when South Africa was finally readmitted to international rugby, that I thought about playing for the Springboks.

As a Jeppe boy, the biggest thing for me was to play for Transvaal and there wasn't a better platform than RAU, whose senior side was captained by Francois Pienaar and coached by Oom Koos Ehlers, a coaching figure as renowned in Johannesburg as Oom Tat Botha was in Bloemfontein.

I'd play for the U21s on the weekend and Koshuis (Residence) rugby on a Wednesday evening. The senior side players would often come down to watch the Koshuis matches and I distinctly recall being chirped from the touchline by the senior team prop, Kapstok van Greuning, who would also go on to play for Transvaal. He had a reputation as a fighter and enforcer, but I wasn't going to stand back. I took the chirp as a challenge and I wanted to battle him next to the field.

Francois, who also had a reputation when I got to RAU as an enforcer and someone who never took a step back in a fight, intervened to defuse the situation. It was the first time he calmed me down on a rugby field but it wouldn't be the last.

I alternated between the U21s and senior RAU side and won the 1992 National Club Championships in Durban alongside an impressive Pienaar and Pieter Hendriks, an electric winger whose pace was unmatched. The tournament felt like a Rugby World Cup in itself which was probably a valuable experience for my two teammates who went on to play pivotal roles in beating Australia in the 1995 World Cup opener at Newlands before Francois famously led the Springboks to the title.

Life was good in 1992 and I was grateful for that. It was so different to the previous year when I had failed to make the adjustment, socially, to being in Bloemfontein.

Work at Little Holland and the casino was keeping me busy, and it has to be said that my mates were always enthusiastic to come and visit me at Little Holland! My rugby was all I could have wished for and I was revelling in the environment at RAU.

I'd taken particular delight from our intervarsity clash against Tukkies at Loftus Versfeld in Pretoria, where I came up against hooker Chris Rossouw for the first time. Chris was highly rated in Northern Transvaal, but on this particular day I schooled him and shot the lights out. It was a game I particularly enjoyed and when he later joined Transvaal, I took every opportunity at training to remind him of that day.

We became teammates in the mid-1990s but I never regarded him as a teammate. We played the same position and that made him my enemy. I caught up with him recently at 1995 World Cup wing James Small's funeral and we had a bit of a laugh about the fire that burned within us back then.

It was a good chat, I think we have both matured. But back in 1992, it certainly wasn't the case and my memory of Transvaal training sessions was the two of us going at each other.

Harry Viljoen was the Transvaal coach in 1992 but he resigned after a heart-breaking 14-13 Currie Cup final defeat against the Sharks at Ellis Park. I only ever played for the U21s during Harry's term in charge of the senior side but when he was succeeded by Kitch I was chosen in the squad for an end-of-season tour of the United Kingdom and Europe.

The Springboks were also touring the northern hemisphere for the first time since readmission, having lost to the All Blacks and Wallabies in South Africa. There were nine or 10 Transvaal players in the Springboks squad and they were excluded from our tour, which would start just after South Africa's final Test of the tour, against England at Twickenham.

Kitch, who had enjoyed a successful club coaching career in

Northern Transvaal, appointed former Transvaal and Springbok winger Ray Mordt as his assistant coach. Ray would be in charge of fitness and skills and his sessions became the stuff of legend, such was the intensity.

Ray was immense as a player. In the 1981 Springbok tour of New Zealand he scored a hat-trick at Eden Park in the final Test of a three-match series against the All Blacks. The Boks went down 25-22 in a match made famous for the bloke who was trying to fly a plane into the stands while dropping flour bombs from the Auckland sky, one of which knocked out All Blacks prop Gary Knight.

Ray was, and is, a gem. I had so much respect for him because of what he achieved as a player but I also had the highest regard for what he brought to a team set-up, be it as an assistant coach or head coach. He's a straight-talker with such passion for the game.

He was a lunatic when it came to fitness, though. He simply fucked us up. We were amateurs in 1992, but Ray had played for Wigan and his approach had that professional rugby league mentality. He wasn't just a fitness coach, he believed in muscle conditioning. Everything that is today taken for granted, in terms of the way pro rugby players approach strength and conditioning, was foreign to most of the guys back then.

I was among the exceptions purely because of my ambition to be a bodybuilder when I was at high school. I was conditioned to weights training because I'd started going to gym when I was in Grade 10. But the way Ray used weights, and combined them with speed training, was just cruel.

We trained nearly every day in 1993 and Ray would take particular delight in using the Wanderers Golf Course fairway, next to our training ground at the Wanderers Rugby Club, as a hill for power sprinting. The 2.4-kilometre run round the course would be the appetiser followed by elevated 200-metre sprints, at least five of them, dropping to 150 metres and then 100 metres.

The only relief, if one could call it that, was the 50-metre sprint!

We got to jog back halfway down the incline, walk the other half and then start all over again. Ray demanded five sets of each. And that was our warm-up.

Then we hit the scrum machine and there was more running from one tryline to the other. It was a case of hit and walk, then lineout practice, then real contact, a bit more running and then we ran 10 pyramids, from tryline to tryline, with a sandbag. It was like having a little oke on your back!

We'd finish off with step-ups on a concrete slab, while holding weights between 2.5 and 7.5 kilograms and then we'd start team training before ending the session with what he called "Ray Mordt's power half-hour of dumbbells".

The sessions lasted up to three hours. It was crazy shit, but I must confess to loving it.

Ray was slightly less intense in his approach to the Lions' 1992 November tour of Europe because we were set to play six matches in three weeks. We lost the first one to Gloucester but won the remaining five and I felt I had rewarded Kitch's faith in me. He had taken a young side on the tour because so many Springboks were absent and we felt we had done well.

But the coach wasn't as impressed as we were and some players who crossed the line in terms of drinking or arriving late for any team meeting, bus departure or training session never represented Transvaal again after that tour.

Kitch didn't tolerate poor discipline and, even though he had so much belief in me, he wouldn't accept anything but my very best. I recall him calling me over after one fitness session, when I finished among the last five, and telling me that I had one chance to fix it in the next series of drills. If I wasn't in the top five, he was sending me home.

Kitch had won the Lion Cup in the last domestic match of 1992 and started the November tour from a position of strength.

If the players thought the overseas tour was reward for winning the Lion Cup, it was quickly clear that this was no year-end wind down but rather a 1993 pre-season tour.

He used the trip to assess younger talent but also to weed out the old legacy players who refused to adapt to his kind of discipline. He also did it very strategically in that he lured several big-name players from Northern Transvaal to join Transvaal in the early part of 1993.

Discipline was everything for Kitch, arriving late wasn't an option. His other pet hates were players running into touch with the ball, or not being able to recycle the ball after being tackled. If you couldn't be on time and you couldn't keep the ball alive, you wouldn't play for his teams.

This was my first experience of Kitch Christie on tour and he was insane when it came to discipline, fitness drills and conditioning. You either called him Coach or Mr Christie but as a player you never called him Kitch. He wasn't there to be anyone's friend and that is where so many of the younger modern coaches get it wrong. I enjoyed that Kitch was an elder statesman, who had done the hard yards and earned the right to be called Mr Christie through a long club coaching career with Harlequins in Pretoria and within the Northern Transvaal coaching structure.

Kitch was unrelenting in his discipline. To ensure that we didn't go overboard on Saturday nights, he had us run at 7am on Sunday mornings. Whether we ran five or 10 kilometres would depend on how he perceived we all looked on our arrival on the Sunday morning, and the quality of our performance and the result of the previous day. Kitch didn't like losing.

The team leadership was also big on initiations. I never agreed with it but I have to admit to finding it very defining on that 1992 tour.

The old generation Afrikaans guys on the tour led the initiation and it was as brutal as it was bizarre.

It works like this: They break you down and humiliate you, then they give you the beating of your life and then they welcome you in to their brotherhood because you have survived it.

The ceremony procedure would start with one of the new players being called up in front of the squad. You would be told to strip naked and you were given butter and then you had to rub your balls anti clockwise and your head clockwise. If you couldn't co-ordinate this, they would bend you over and beat your arse. While this is going on you have to down beers and do boat races.

Once you got through this, they'd make you get off the chair and pick up a bottle of beer with your arse. I just couldn't do this and found it hilarious that such an emphasis was put on this. Then I saw why. Once the initiated new guy had completed the beer bottle pick-up, the senior men would bring in the next new guy and make them watch the final act of the other new guy's initiation. This involved lying on a flat surface on our back and looking up at the players as they sang the team song. Halfway through the team song, they'd flip you over and beat your back and arse. They hit me so hard the table broke.

They'd then welcome you to the team and instruct the next new player to drink from the very same beer bottle that had been picked up with a player's arse. It was disgusting but at that point, in a primal and crass way, I felt I actually belonged and I felt part of this brotherhood. I felt I was officially a Transvaal player.

I believe in change and so much has changed in South African rugby when it comes to culture and traditions. But not all that was old was bad and while the initiation was extreme, so much of today's team initiations are sanitised and soulless.

The initiation finally made me feel an acceptance and belonging, which could also tell you more about my need to feel accepted and to be a part of something. The 1992 overseas tour was also the first time I experienced Francois Pienaar's on-field presence and leadership in a first-class environment. It was different level.

Francois was an incredibly inspirational captain. He would lead by example. He had a very assertive way of carrying his message across. Some captains would be all verbal or all action, but Francois had both and he commanded respect, within the team and from the opposition.

He had done it tough as a youngster, but already on the 1992 tour you could see his maturity under the guidance of Kitch. Francois and Kitch agreed that strength of discipline was going to be key if we wanted to have success and I found Francois to be a captain who could relate to the young players as easily as he did the older generation. There was no doubt, even among the older guys, that Francois was the captain.

The tour was about the future and not the past. Some players didn't respond well to the discipline demands but it resonated with me. I was a better tourist and player in an environment where I knew exactly what and when something was expected of me. I thrived on structure.

Kitch gave me the nickname "Bullet" at one of our initial training sessions under him. It was the Rolls Royce of nicknames. I didn't know why he chose that name and I never asked him. I just accepted it. I was "Bullet" to him and he was "Coach" to me. We had an instant understanding of each other and my respect for him never waned.

I thought I had done enough on the tour to convince Kitch that I should be his starting hooker in 1993. I desperately wanted to be part of the inaugural Super 10 competition (featuring teams from South Africa, Australia, New Zealand and Samoa) because the Springboks were scheduled to make their first tour of Australia since readmission and I felt I was good enough to make the squad.

My confidence was high when the tour ended and we returned home but I was disappointed to find out that Kitch had persuaded Uli Schmidt to leave Northern Transvaal (now the Bulls) and play for Transvaal.

Uli had spent his entire career at Northern Transvaal and was the most revered hooker of his generation in South African rugby. He is one of those rugby talents that, in his prime, would have counted among the best in the world but South African rugby was in sporting isolation when Uli was at his most lethal.

I thought 1993 would be my time and it jarred my confidence that Kitch had felt it necessary to turn to Uli. On reflection, it gave me the greatest apprenticeship in 1993 because, on a weekly basis, I was testing myself against a player of Uli's class, and he went on to show just how much class he had with a massive performance in the Super 10 final against Auckland, which Transvaal won 20-17. Uli also scored the match-winning try in the Lion Cup and was instrumental in Transvaal winning the Currie Cup.

Even though I felt I should be starting, Uli's performances ensured that it was never a discussion when it came to team selection. Uli had made it clear that he only wanted to play his rugby under Kitch and he made himself unavailable for Springbok selection in 1993, so my domestic playing opportunities were limited.

Kitch never spoke to me about an apprenticeship role and I am sure he never asked Uli to look after me or mentor me. It wasn't Kitch's way. The two of us just had to get on with it, like I had to get on with it when Chris Rossouw also made the move from Northern Transvaal to Transvaal.

Uli wasn't small and he wasn't big either, but he was fucking hard. His dad, Louis, was considered a Northern Transvaal ironman and Uli's upbringing was as uncompromising as they come.

Uli wasn't going anywhere in 1993 and I had no option but to front at every training session and support Kitch's decision to invest in South Africa's most celebrated hooker of the mid-1980s and early 1990s.

Uli didn't ignore me at training and he offered insights but he certainly wasn't there to develop me as a player. He was there to prove he was number one, so I had to be on my game because he came at me in live scrums. We'd ram each other at the scrum engage, and if I was relaxed or arrogant, and didn't respect the challenge, I'd get hurt. He mentored me by way of his approach.

Uli was a class act as a rugby player and I would certainly rank him in the top three to five in the world in overall skill, physicality, presence, scrumming technique, ball-carrying and mental toughness. He had a tenacity and defiance that was superior to most and he was one of the brightest rugby players I ever met. If he wasn't playing rugby or working as a doctor he was studying for some or other degree.

From a rugby perspective, 1993 was strange in that I was part of the best provincial team in the world but rarely got to experience their brilliance on the field. Like the other reserves, I had the best view in the stands but it wasn't always a view I enjoyed.

Francois was colossal in 1993 and the Super 10 final win against an Auckland team full of All Blacks highlighted the class of the Transvaal team.

I may not have enjoyed the view but I was awed by the quality of player I could call a teammate. All of those players would be stars in the modern game.

The pack was monstrous and prop Balie Swart, locks Kobus Wiese and Hannes Strydom would all start the 1995 World Cup opener against Australia. By then Uli, Heinrich Rogers and Johan le Roux, the 1993 front row regulars, had all retired. Francois captained Transvaal in 1993 and the Springboks at the 1995 World Cup, while Rudolf Straeuli played in the World Cup final. The hardened flank veterans of Ian Macdonald and Deon Lotter didn't make it to the World Cup in 1995 but they both got to play for the Springboks.

Our backs were potent. Pieter Hendriks and Gavin Johnson, were in the back three while Japie Mulder, so good in the 1995

World Cup final, was in the midfield. Halfbacks Johan Roux and Hennie le Roux would also experience World Cup success. The 1993 Transvaal team shared the M-Net Night Series, won the Lion Cup and won the Currie Cup for the first time since 1972.

I was officially a part of the squad but it didn't feel like it because I'd either be on the bench or in the stands, close to the team but not yet an established regular within it.

But I refused to let it detract from my rugby year. I was privileged to train, learn from and contribute to what was a magnificent squad of players. Sometimes, one only recognises class and quality in hindsight, but in 1993 you had to be blind not to know instantly just how good these players were and how very good they would become.

I counted myself among this group who would flourish as Springboks and, between 1994 and 1998, I backed this up with 31 wins in 34 Springbok Tests, the most special of them being against the Wallabies, then world champions, in the 1995 World Cup opener at Newlands.

FROM BOY TO MAN IN 1994

Francois Pienaar's assertion to the media that the 1993 Transvaal Currie Cup and Super 10-winning team was a better one than the Springboks was a controversial statement, but it wasn't wrong. Francois made the statement based on the continuity in selection of Transvaal, as opposed to the constant chopping and changing of the Springboks. He also made it because of the quality of that Transvaal team, the core of which won the 1995 World Cup for the Springboks. The World Cup win, with so many of those 1993 Transvaal players, vindicated Francois' views.

It is true that many of the great Crusaders line-ups of the professional era would often have been a more difficult prospect than an All Blacks team made up of the best Kiwi players from the five Super Rugby franchises. Many a great international coach has said the best Test XV is not necessarily made up of a nation's best 15 players.

My first introduction to the Springboks was in 1994 and although I only made my Test debut later in the year under Kitch Christie, my first experience of the Boks was earlier in the season when Ian McIntosh was still the coach. McIntosh was on a hiding to nothing on the tour of New Zealand in 1994. Unlike Rassie Erasmus, Mac was one of several selectors and never had the final say on his touring squad, let alone his Test and midweek starting XV. Everyone seemed to have a say and there was a lot of horse-trading that went on. The players knew it, the tour captains knew it and Mac knew it.

It was a different era of rugby when teams were picked by committee, and selections were sometimes based on paybacks or because someone owed someone else a favour. Concessions were made and in return there was future reward because South African rugby's administration was closer to a political than a sporting environment.

I liked Mac from the outset. What you saw is what you got. He was old school, a salt-of-the-earth kind of guy and you knew where you stood with him. If he liked you and was impressed with your performance, be it in training or a match, he referred to you as "master". If he didn't like you or didn't rate your performance, then you were simply called "cunt". It was the Mac way and I could relate to him. He had incredible passion for the teams he coached and he was a players' type of coach. With Mac you only had to look at his eyes to know what he was thinking.

I found him approachable in the 1994 season he coached the Springboks but I found him too passive in presence when it came to asserting himself with the Springbok manager Jannie Engelbrecht, whose claim to fame was a Test career in which the illusion of what he had achieved was far more impressive than the reality. Engelbrecht's teams won 19 out of the 34 Tests he played in, which is a 62-percent win record, but after listening to Jannie talk about his career you'd have thought he'd never played in a losing Springboks team.

Touring for Jannie was more about selling his wine and charming women than it was about the Boks. He was a manager who was all about himself and his decisions never took the players into consideration. If the team found itself based in a weird location, you could be sure it was because Jannie was having a wine exhibition or had done some kind of deal with the locals for the Springboks to be there.

Engelbrecht had a public persona the opposite of Mac's. He was flamboyant and traded on having been a Springbok rugby player with a "legacy" that didn't quite measure up when you started tracking the archives.

Mac, having coached Natal (now the Sharks) all his life, naturally had a bias towards his provincial players, and in 1994, just two years after South Africa's international rugby return, there were provincial cliques and divisions within the Bok squad because of the strength of provincialism. Isolation had divided the nation along provincial lines and the top five teams had each replaced national pride with a provincial identity.

Mac's leaning towards the Natal players he knew was no different to any Bok coach I played under who had strong ties with a provincial union as a coach or player.

This provincial bias among coaches continued long after I retired. Look at Heyneke Meyer at the 2015 World Cup. Meyer had won a Super Rugby title with the Bulls and coached them for a decade and he just couldn't acknowledge the quality of the 2014 and 2015 Lions teams that won the Currie Cup and became South Africa's best Super Rugby team in 2016, 2017 and 2018. Meyer did not select a Lions player in his World Cup squad, yet they were hammering every team in South Africa. Provincialism proved to be Meyer's Achilles heel, his selections were his undoing.

In June of 1994, Mac was given a squad for the incoming series against England, which South Africa drew 1-1 after the disappointment of the first-Test defeat against the Poms in Pretoria.

Francois' comment that Transvaal were a stronger line-up also had merit when you think of how the Transvaal team beat

England at Ellis Park, only for the Springboks to take a beating at Loftus Versfeld one week later.

The English, who arrived with a lot of hype, lost against settled Free State and Natal combinations, edged a second-rate Western Transvaal by two points and lost to a South African XV in Kimberley that enjoyed the luxury of many tried-and-tested combinations.

One of those combinations was the tighthead/hooker duo of Transvaal strong man Johan le Roux and myself. I had been in the Transvaal set-up for two seasons and, even though I was still the emerging kid playing in the shadow of the legendary Uli Schmidt, I had trained with Johan enough to form a rapport. I'd done enough during my opportunities to play for Transvaal to convince the many selectors of my national potential.

I went from playing schools rugby in 1990, and U20 rugby in 1991 and 1992, to facing England's best in 1994. I was riding that youthful crest that makes you feel immortal and untouchable. I was part of a Transvaal team that beat England at Ellis Park on the Saturday and an SA XV that beat England in Kimberley the following Tuesday.

England won just one of their first five matches on that tour, which is why the first Test win against the Springboks in Pretoria was such as shock. "How?" you may ask. Provincial loyalties were so strong and national unity in the context of playing for South Africa was still a foreign concept.

Order was restored in the second Test in Cape Town, but the win was more down to every South African player's refusal to lose at home for a second successive time to England.

If England had been underestimated and disrespected, then the approach to being in New Zealand the following month was the antithesis for every player selected. There was as much trepidation in going to New Zealand as there was excitement, and it was a tour the generations that came before us talked up the most.

There was reverence for the All Blacks and touring New Zealand, and when I got there, I also experienced a similar awe from older All Blacks about their pre-isolation tours of South Africa.

The Springbok touring squad was a strange one, you could see that the selectors had not been on the same page with their opinions and judgements on players. Many of the omissions didn't make sense and neither did a lot of the squad inclusions.

We were going to have to survive more on individual talent, instinct and athleticism because there wasn't much confidence from within the different provincial factions that there was a desire to put nation before province.

I can't overstate the power of provincialism back then, as opposed to today's united Springboks. The coach's provincial background would greatly influence a player's Test prospects on tour if the coach was prepared to fight with selectors to have the player start.

It shocked me when the brilliant Natal fullback Andre Joubert was dropped for the second Test in Wellington and I still don't know how Mac let that happen because there was no way he didn't rate Jouba as his number one fullback.

Mac wasn't as charitable when it came to the hooker situation. I knew Natal's John Allan was Mac's go-to hooker. John had played for Scotland but mostly his career had been in the colours of Natal (now the Sharks). He was Mac's boy and I have always thought it was one of the reasons Uli Schmidt opted out of the tour of New Zealand.

Uli, in his prime, was without comparison in South African rugby as a hooker and he was also among the world's elite. But he would have felt uncertainty about the impact provincialism would play when it came to Springbok selection. The one thing about Uli is he didn't play second fiddle to anyone, and if he felt there was a possibility of exclusion, for whatever reason, he wouldn't risk it. He would rather opt out.

Whatever Uli's reasons, he wasn't in New Zealand for the first Bok tour of New Zealand since international readmission. I was, and so was John Allan.

Given my character and the belief I have always had in my playing ability, I felt I should be the starting Test hooker, but I never expected it to happen because Mac trusted John as a person and as a player. Understanding why Mac opted for John didn't mean I agreed with it. John was a hooker I didn't rate. He had aggression and plenty of passion but he didn't have good skills and the most impressive part of his game was the way he used to charge out of the change-room, down the tunnel and onto the field.

I'd like to have seen John's face on that tour but all I saw were the laces of his size 11's hanging from Mac's backside. Please read that in the spirit intended - it's written with no malice, but more out of laughter because that was the hopelessness of my Test selection situation.

I didn't hold it against Mac because I know loyalty and I respect those who have loyalty. What Mac showed John was loyalty.

Mac loved John and early on in the tour at training he told me to learn from John in how to throw the ball with two hands at the lineout. I was young, insulted and irritated. As Mac walked away, with his back turned to me, I vented my frustration by hurling the ball at him. True to form, I missed and Mac didn't have to say anything more. He would have felt he had made his point and I had only justified it with the inaccuracy of my throw.

It wasn't one of my finer moments but I immediately saw the funny side of it, and when you tour New Zealand the only escape is laughter, even if at your own expense.

I warmed the bench in the three-Test series against the All Blacks and in those days the biggest risk of injury to the reserves would be splinters to one's arse. You only got on if there was blood or if a player was hurt so badly that he couldn't continue.

There were no substitutions, players were expected to start and finish a match. I knew it would take a miracle for me to get a Test opportunity in New Zealand but I also knew I was going to experience the full might of the New Zealand domestic game, which was comfortably the strongest in the world.

I had travelled to New Zealand with Transvaal's Super Rugby team earlier that year and played against Horowhenua while Uli had played the second game against North Harbour. This was my first experience of New Zealand as a rugby country, though. We toured from the top of the North Island to the most southern tip. It felt like we had to do it in a day, when the tour actually lasted nearly two months.

It remains the toughest and most demanding challenge I've ever experienced as a rugby player. New Zealand is a beautiful country and there are few places with such natural scenic beauty but the operational side of touring there in 1994 was very different.

As players in South Africa, we were used to seeing golden sunshine but in New Zealand it was all grey. We discovered the difference between a motel and a hotel, between a motorway and a highway and what it really meant to play rugby in wet weather. The renowned Cape winters in South Africa wouldn't even register at New Zealand's weather bureau.

Playing conditions were difficult, the travel was tedious and taxing and the rugby was the hardest I'd ever encountered. Say what you want about the Kiwis, love them, hate them, worship them or be repulsed by them, there is no greater place to play rugby.

There is no harder examination of one as a rugby player and in my entire career I never played in a tougher match than the 19-12 defeat to Otago at Carisbrook. I have also not felt such an intimidating atmosphere. Otago were the first and only provincial team to beat us on the 1994 tour and the reward for them was the handing over of the tour Springbok head.

Provincial and club teams historically coveted being the first to get the Springbok head on tours and the Boks had lost their head to Canterbury in 1921, to Waikato in 1956 and to Wellington in 1965. Otago had been incredible in taking the British and Irish Lions tour head on four occasions and on 27th July, 1994 they finally got our Springbok head.

I hated playing in a team that would give up the Springbok head but there are times in sport where you don't lose a game but are beaten by a better opponent. Otago on that day were just too strong, too skilled and too good.

I remember the cold from that day and the rain that preceded the match, where there had been two days of continual rain. I also remember Joost van der Westhuizen charging down flyhalf Stephen Bachop's first kick of the match to score less than 20 seconds into the match. More than anything I won't forget the ferocity of the Otago players and the heroics of their captain and hooker, David Latta. My understanding is Latta was an iconic figure in Otago but because he played in the Sean Fitzpatrick era he never got to wear the All Blacks No 2 jersey. I can tell you, if he was playing in the modern era, he'd have worn black with the same impact he wore the blue and gold of Otago.

Latta, the media wrote the next day, had played his greatest ever game for Otago. A young 20-year-old named Jeff Wilson also kicked five from six, while Hennie le Roux struggled with the conditions and could only convert one from six attempts at goal.

Goal-kicking didn't cost us the game, though.

Latta, like the Otago players, was gracious in victory and that is one thing I have always admired about the Kiwi players. When they beat you there is very little post-match arrogance and when they get beaten there is only congratulations for you being the better team on the day. It is what makes the South African and New Zealand rivalry so special.

There was a part of me that felt I had contributed to failing the legend of the Springboks in New Zealand because we lost to Otago but there was also a part that felt I could talk with certainty about the challenge of touring New Zealand, beyond playing the All Blacks.

Modern players will never know how it feels to trek up and down the north and south islands of New Zealand for two months and play twice a week. The physical challenge of those provincial players was unrelenting and the tour itself was mentally draining but I had grown immeasurably as a rugby player and one of the touring South African journalists, Barney Spender, wrote in the *Mail and Guardian* newspaper that I was one of the forwards who had advanced my international career on the tour.

"Dalton began the tour, socks around his ankles and catapult in pocket, with the brash petulance of a schoolboy gang-leader. But when he settled down and concentrated on playing rugby, he showed that he really is a footballer with huge potential," wrote Spender.

I don't know about the reference to the schoolboy gang-leader but I read it as a compliment that I had made the necessary impact, even though it didn't earn me a Test start. Mac persisted with John Allan, despite the back-to-back defeats in Dunedin and Wellington. I found it difficult to deal with the frustration of being on the bench pre-professional rugby in 1996 because of the unlikelihood of getting a game.

In 1994 I warmed the bench in 10 Tests: two against England, three against the All Blacks, two against Argentina and in three on the November tour to the United Kingdom. I got five minutes in the first Test against Argentina in Port Elizabeth, which would be my Test debut. Those five minutes in 1994 were the exception to the reserve hooker rule that I would invariably see little on-field Test action.

I always wanted to start and felt I was good enough to start from the moment I was promoted from the U21 squad to the seniors. In fact, as a youngster in 1992, I even introduced myself to the Bok coach, John Williams, when he walked past me in the tunnel at Loftus Versfeld. I went over to him, shook his hand and told him my name was James Dalton and that I was his next Springbok hooker. He looked perplexed and a bit dumbfounded and I can't recall him even responding.

I would end my Springbok career in 2002, having started 40 of my 43 Tests and as the starting hooker in all 15 non-Test matches. I take great pride in that statistic and feel I have been true to my boast to Williams, even if in 1994 I only had five precious Test minutes to show from a possible 800.

I knew my time would come but I must confess to lacking the patience to wait, as was the case against the All Blacks in New Zealand in 1994.

The hardest part of the series against the All Blacks was dealing with the excitement of possibly getting on and then having to stomach the disappointment of not playing. I always found myself in two minds, trying to get involved mentally in the match because an injury could happen, but getting more and more disillusioned and feeling powerless to influence the outcome. In those Test matches, I felt I was more of a spectator than a player.

The first Test in Dunedin could easily have gone our way and it was more one we lost than they won. But the second Test, played at the old Athletic Park in Wellington, was one in which we were hanging on for scoreboard credibility instead of pushing for victory to level the series.

In my time I have played on a few dodgy pitches and changed in a few dungeons that doubled as a change room, but there was nothing more archaic as a Test venue than Athletic Park. I hated being there and, in 1994, I would never have thought I'd be back at the same ground four years later to experience one of the most famous Test wins against the All Blacks.

The elation after the 1998 win against New Zealand was very

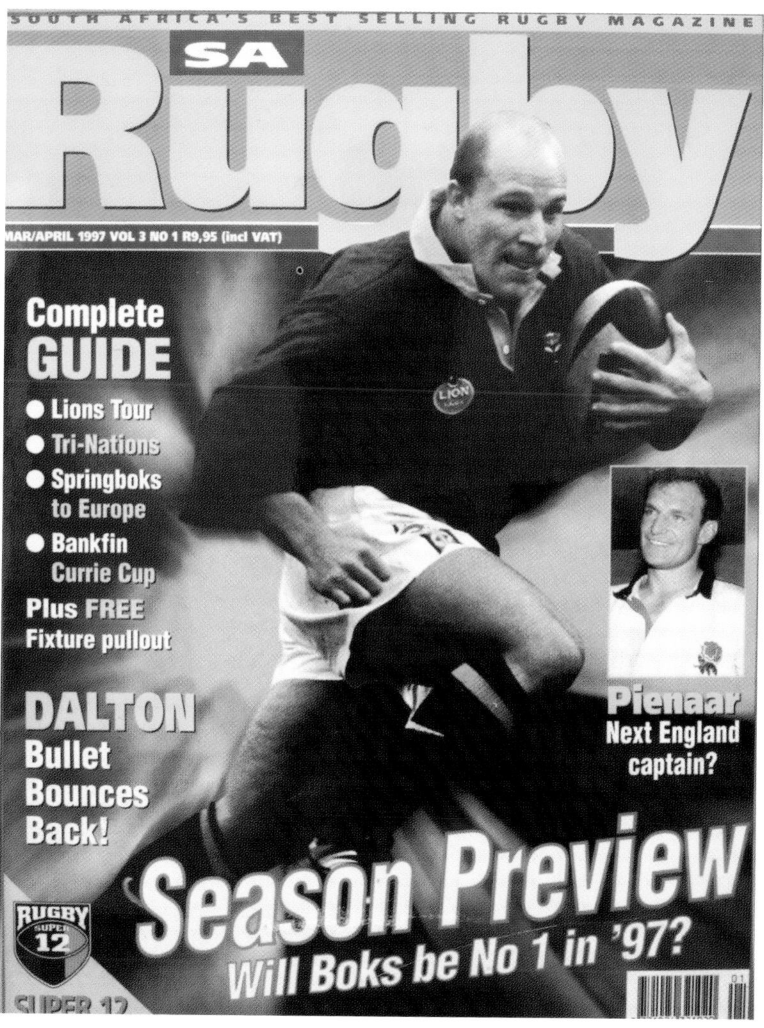
SOUTH AFRICA'S BEST SELLING RUGBY MAGAZINE
SA
Rugby
MAR/APRIL 1997 VOL 3 NO 1 R9,95 (incl VAT)
Complete
GUIDE
Lions Tour
Tri-Nations
Springboks to Europe
Bankfin Currie Cup
Plus FREE Fixture pullout
DALTON
Bullet Bounces Back!
Pienaar
Next England captain?
Season Preview
Will Boks be No 1 in '97?
RUGBY SUPER 12
SUPER 12

My life from schoolboy to Springbok in pictures. Check out the hair on that youngster!

Contiues on next page

DALTON
vodacom

Holding the Webb Ellis Cup with Springbok captain Francois Pienaar during the parade that followed South Africa winning the 1995 Rugby World Cup.

RANDSE AFRIKAANSE UNIVERSITEIT
EERSTE RUGBYSPAN - 1992
WENNERS TOYOTA KLUB KAMPIOENSKAP

The team photograph of the 1992 RAU side that won the Club Championship

TOP: Posing for a photo with Springbok teammate Adrian Garvey at a team function.
BELOW: Sharing the World Cup trophy with my friends (from left) Camillo, Bruno and Italo.

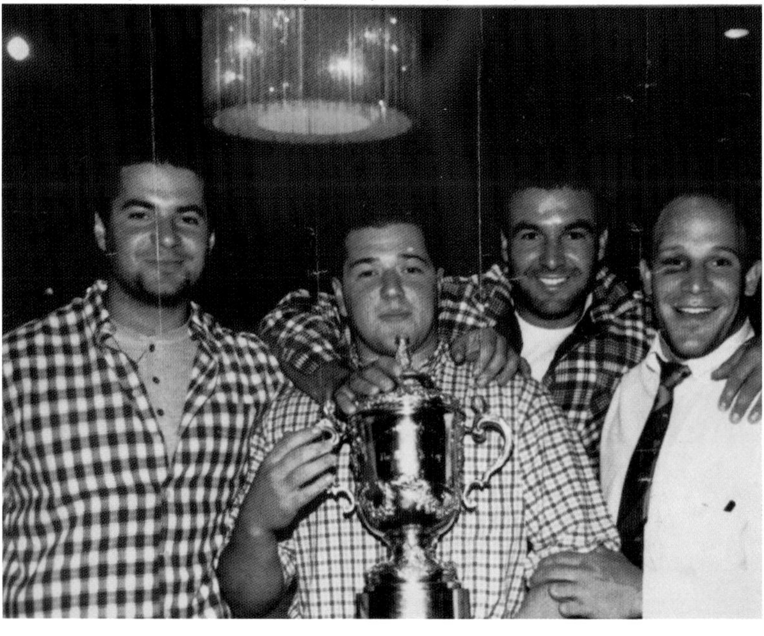

TOP: In between Adrian Garvey (L) and Dawie Theron (R) after a win on tour at the end of 1996.
BELOW: Relaxing in the change room after a 1996 tour victory with Henry Honiball (L), Adrian Garvey and Ruben Kruger (R).

TOP: Celebrating a big win against Argentina in Buenos Aires in 1996 with (from left to right) Toks van der Linde, Kobus Wiese, Adrian Garvey and Henry Tromp.
BELOW: Trying a few French snacks during the 1996 tour with (from left to right) assistant coach Hugh Reece-Edwards, Kevin Putt and Adrian Garvey.

TOP: Waiting with Adrian Garvey and Mark Andrews (R) for the bus to take us on a team activity in Bordeaux during the 1996 tour of Europe.
BELOW: The front row of Os du Randt (right), myself and Adrian Garvey (left) after a 29-11 win against England at Twickenham in November of 1997. Garvey scored a try in that match.

TOP: Posing for a photo before the captain's run at Twickenham in 1997 with (from left to right) Andrew Aitken, picked to make his first Test start, Adrian Garvey and assistant coach Alan Solomons.
BELOW: Enjoying Europe in 1997 with my travel buddy, Adrian Garvey.

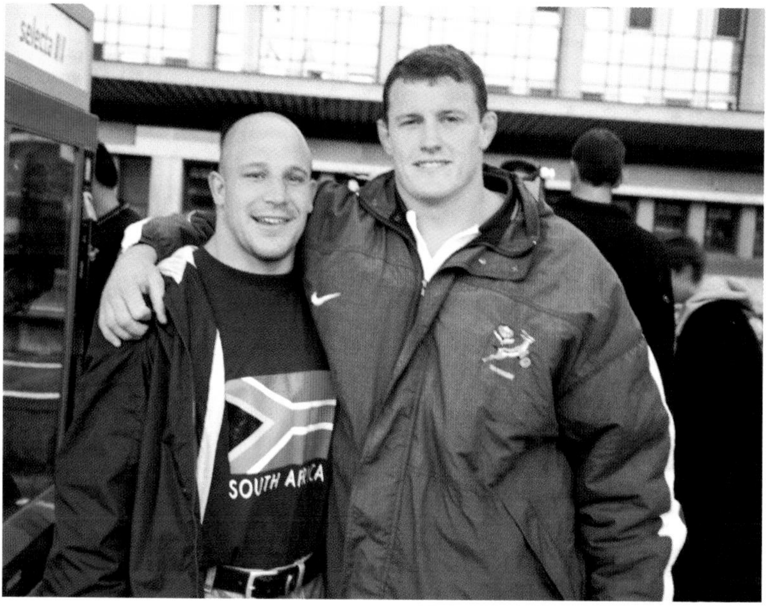

TOP: Touring can be fun and here there's lots of nervous smiles from Hannes Strydom and (in front) Adrian Garvey and Japie Mulder - I made sure that if this rollercoaster derailed, my gold chain was coming with me!
BELOW: As you can see from me sharing a post-match bath with Andre Venter, the recovery process was a little bit less scientific in the late 90s.

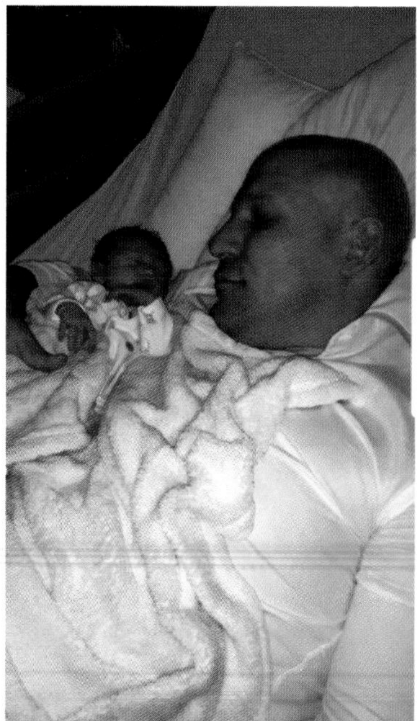

TOP LEFT: Claire and my daughter Mila ready to open some Christmas presents.
TOP RIGHT: A precious catnap with my newborn daughter Mila.
BELOW: HO-HO-HO! I put the "father" in Father Christmas with my son Daniel itching to unwrap his presents.

TOP: A fun photoshoot with "Bully Junior", my son Daniel.
BELOW: It doesn't get any better than a kiss from my daughter, Mila.

TOP LEFT: Reunited with the trophy and Francois Pienaar at the 1995 Springboks' 20-year reunion in London.
TOP RIGHT: Catching up with (from left to right) Naka Drotske, Chris Rossouw and Ireland hooker Keith Wood at the reunion.
BOTTOM LEFT: Before a game for the J9 Foundation in Dubai, Claire and baby Mila pose for a picture with my legendary 1995 Rugby World Cup teammate, Joost van der Westhuizen.
BOTTOM RIGHT: Great to see, among others, Chester Williams and Japie Mulder at the 20-year reunion of the 1995 world champions.
Thank you!

different to what the entire squad felt after the 13-9 defeat in 1994. It was awful to know the series was lost when there was still one Test and two provincial matches to play, with one of those provincial matches being the Otago defeat a few days after the low of Wellington.

More than the defeat against the All Blacks, my memory of Wellington will always be the sending home of our prop Johan le Roux for biting the ear of All Blacks captain Sean Fitzpatrick. It really was more a nibble than a bite and it followed typical Fitzpatrick provocation and gamesmanship, which eventually forced him to retaliate.

The way the Springbok management treated Johan was disgraceful and I don't think he will ever forgive them for throwing him to the wolves that were the New Zealand media and New Zealand public.

We, as a squad, had just lost the series, and the controversy around Johan could have galvanised the squad had the management leadership of Mac and Jannie Engelbrecht backed him. I know Francois was called in as captain and that he ultimately had to support the decision to send Johan home but Francois has gone on record to say it is one of his biggest ever regrets as a Springbok captain.

Johan was treated like a convict and abruptly ex-communicated from the squad. I was his roommate and I couldn't believe the treatment and the coldness with which it was done.

He was a hard man, tough as they come, and one who thrived on loyalty. He was an enforcer in any team he played, as dirty as the most revered international props of that era, and a player who could take as good a punch as he threw. Rugby, in that generation, wasn't sanitised and your front row forwards were expected to handle more than a right or left shoulder on the scrum engage.

As players in the squad we didn't know the exact detail of what had transpired the night after the Test, but we refused to accept how easily the coach and manager could give up on him and alienate him from his teammates while still in New Zealand.

Johan had been trialled by media and his own management and, less than 24 hours after giving everything for his country, he had been banished from all rugby for 18 months. He was crushed and would never recover, and when he most needed his teammates, the management had excluded him from a team social boat trip immediately after his suspension.

It caused such unhappiness within the squad and it didn't make for the ideal preparation for our trip to Dunedin to play Otago. The players felt let down by the management because he had been betrayed in a moment that demanded support, patriotism and loyalty.

Instead, he got nothing of the sort and was left on his own in Wellington. I will never forget the look on his face as the team bus headed out: he stood behind the bus, his expression one of disbelief, as we drove to the next location. All the players on the bus were hurting watching him stand there alone. It was gut-wrenching to watch this mountain of a man being reduced to an infant, such was the humiliation he must have felt.

Johan le Roux had been sacrificed without a fight from within our own leadership, who continued to insult him by making him pay for his own legal defence. They also banned him from wearing his Springboks blazer on the flight back to South Africa.

New Zealand is famous for being a graveyard to many international rugby careers, and this was especially true in the days of tours, but Johan's Test career should never have ended with a blow to the head from his own team management.

Francois, as captain, was appalled by the management's decision and he rallied the boys to finish the tour as a tribute to Johan. Unfortunately, our response to Otago's challenge was as effective as the management's was to Johan's plight.

We would lose to Otago, which was our only provincial defeat in 11 non-Test matches, and the Test team would score two tries to nil in drawing the final Test of the series 18-18 at Auckland's Eden Park. It all seemed so hollow.

Today, most teams would consider it gold to tour New Zealand and lose three in 14. The British and Irish Lions won five from 10 matches in 2017 and lost one, drew won and won one Test against an All Blacks team reduced to 14 players after 25 minutes in Wellington. It is regarded as one of the greatest British and Irish Lions tours, yet our 1994 effort was described in the media as a disaster, and the President of South African Rugby Doc Louis Luyt went public to say he wanted Mac removed before we had even left New Zealand.

By the time we got home, Mac had been fired.

SEEING RED IN P.E.

Port Elizabeth's Boet Erasmus Stadium is where I made my Test debut against Argentina in 1994, but if that five-minute cameo made me think of the Boet as my field of Springbok dreams, then the night of our 1995 World Cup match against Canada at the same venue turned it into my house of horrors.

It is where my World Cup ended and I got sent off for the first and only time in 58 Springboks matches, including 43 Tests.

And I didn't even throw a punch!

It is also the red card that just seems to refuse to go away and it was even used as motivation and justification for my alleged danger as a father to my son.

If you weren't at the Boet that night or weren't watching the game, it is on YouTube. There are a few versions and it doesn't matter which angle is used, it is clear that I never punched anyone and my crime was to rush in to stop a fight that started when Canada's fullback, Scott Stewart, threw Springbok left wing Pieter Hendriks into the advertising boards.

It had been a particularly messy night because Canada knew they had no chance of beating us, so the approach of the Canadians was to play us off the ball and to slow the game down at every possible turn. The match lacked pace and intensity but that doesn't mean it was a difficult match. We had all the ball and they made a record number of tackles. We were in total control of a match that was more nasty than brutal because of the many off-the-ball incidents.

Then Stewart had a go at Pieter, I ran in to separate the two and I got swung over the advertising boards. By the time I got up, Pieter had kicked a Canadian player, Joost van der Westhuizen and Hennie le Roux had thrown punches that had landed and our lock Hannes Strydom was leaving the field with blood oozing from his face.

Several players could have been sent off for the fight but only Canada prop Rod Snow was singled out for throwing punches. Irish referee David McHugh told Bok captain Francois Pienaar that International Rugby Union regulations determined that, as a referee, he had to identify the third man in because it was the view of the lawmakers that the third man in would set off a bigger fight.

Francois pleaded my innocence with McHugh and in his book *Rainbow Warrior* documents his exchange with McHugh as one in which he appealed vehemently and emotionally for me not to be sent off.

"He was trying to stop the fight," said Francois. "He didn't even throw a punch. Come on, referee. We came to play rugby and they came to fight. Let's keep things in perspective. He'll be banned from the tournament."

I knew this wasn't going to be an exchange in which Francois' charisma could triumph. McHugh was defiant in his decision and I knew I was in trouble, even though I had not struck a Canadian player.

I put my two hands on my head, looked to the heavens and remember asking 'why?'

Why now? Why me?

What now?

I had to go, my match was over and I knew the potential of

my World Cup going the same way was more a probability than a possibility.

The night had been an ugly one from the start. The floodlights failed during the national anthems and kick-off had to be delayed by 45 minutes, which meant the match had only finished after 11 in the evening.

The walk back to the tunnel felt as long as the drive from Port Elizabeth to Johannesburg, and I had this awful feeling that the evening was only going to get worse. I didn't watch the final minutes of the Test but sat in the change room distraught at what had just happened. The tears flowed, just like they would when I addressed the media a few days later.

Some mocked me and cussed at me for crying, but the majority cuddled me. In 1995, playing in the World Cup in South Africa was all that mattered to me. It was all that had consumed me in the six-month build-up to the tournament opener against Australia in Cape Town.

I had never been in better shape physically and mentally and with Uli Schmidt having retired, this was my year to make a statement that I was the number one hooker in the country, and the world.

That opening fortnight of the World Cup had been epic. I'd never experienced national support on such a large scale and I don't know if there is an adjective to do justice to the emotion that I felt in the early part of the World Cup.

We'd got to meet President Nelson Mandela, who had visited us at training at the South African Defence Force's Silvermine fields in Cape Town, and I had got to measure myself against one of the world's best hookers in Australia's Phil Kearns.

I was buzzing when we arrived in Port Elizabeth for the Canadian match, but by the time McHugh had blown the final whistle, all the fizz was out of me.

Francois, in *Rainbow Warrior*, described me as a player who looked miserable and broken after the match. He wasn't wrong. Francois is an inspirational leader and thrived on positivity, but even he knew there was nothing he could say to me in the change room. Frankly, in those moments, there is nothing to say.

We had won our third pool match and qualified for the quarter-finals, but there was no celebrating in the change room. I was told there would be a disciplinary at the stadium before I left.

The South African Rugby Union president Doc Luyt wanted to get legal opinion and a legal representative for me. Doc was very supportive and told me we could win this thing. I wanted to believe him but there was so much emotion going on in the hour after the match and there seemed to be an urgency from our team manager Morne du Plessis to get the disciplinary over with, so the team could focus on the quarter-final.

Morne declined Doc Luyt's offer and felt that it would prejudice me if we went in with lawyers. The game in 1995 was still amateur and Morne believed that rugby people should be handling rugby matters. Morne, one of the best players of his generation and respected globally as an ambassador of the sport, underestimated what we would be walking into at the disciplinary. I wanted legal representation; I didn't agree with him then and I don't agree with him today. I felt we could have handled the situation better and the haste with which everything was agreed meant I was more a lamb going to the slaughter than a rugby player heading to a disciplinary with any chance of success.

The disciplinary happened around midnight and it didn't last long. Two of the three-man panel were French-speaking and we had to wait for the French interpreter before we could start. When I spoke in defence of my actions, however, my English was never translated into French. Throughout the brief judiciary, there was no French spoken and the entire proceeding was one-sided and weighted against me. I was always going to be found guilty by these so-called rugby people, who in that moment, were a law unto themselves and were never going to be challenged on any technical aspects of their finding. I was given a 30-day suspension and my World Cup was over. Kitch spoke with me when we got back to the hotel in the early hours of Sunday morning and he was sympathetic and empathetic. He told me I was the number one hooker in the squad and that wouldn't change after the World Cup. He told me I was influential in us beating Australia at Newlands and that I had been very effective in my hassling of scrumhalf George Gregan. He also felt I had won the individual battle against Kearns. He said I would have to be strong emotionally because it wasn't going to be easy watching the squad in the play-offs but he wanted me to know that I was a part of the World Cup and when the Springboks won the World Cup, he would ensure I got my gold medal.

The coach, as always, was true to his word. The Springboks won the World Cup and the first time the team played as world champions, against Wales at Ellis Park in September of 1995, Kitch picked me as his starting hooker.

I'd also start in the season's final Test when we beat England at Twickenham.

DAWN OF THE PRO ERA

Doc Louis Luyt, former Transvaal and then South African Rugby Union president, had an incredible presence about him but also kept his distance. He was the paymaster, the players were the puppets and he would tell us when and how to dance. He had the authority to make a decision to include you or exclude you.

You watched your dance steps around him and you watched your Ps and Qs. There were so many different sides to Doc Luyt, but the one I related to most was that he was the man who signed our pay cheques.

Prior to the 1995 World Cup, rugby was an amateur sport and there were no official payments. Doc Luyt was quite creative in circumventing this and ensuring there was something for his Currie Cup champions. We'd get a monthly retainer of about R7500, and R2000 in cash for every match played. The cash would be given to us in an envelope. This was for Transvaal provincial matches, and if you played club rugby, it was considerably less for a match fee and there was no such thing as a club rugby player retainer.

If you weren't at university or in the military or police force, you had to have a job to support your passion for playing the game at a club or provincial level.

The sport was strictly amateur but in the early 1990s, the way

Doc Luyt ran the union was very professional. He was among the most influential role players in helping the sport turn pro and he has not been given his due for what he did for the game in South Africa and internationally, and for expediting the transition to professionalism in 1996. He was the architect of uniting South Africa, New Zealand and Australia in the original Tri-Nations Test Championship and in the Super 12 provincial and regional competition, which in its original guise, was without comparison in world rugby.

I always enjoyed Doc Luyt and I had huge respect for his authority as the leader of the union and also for what he had achieved in life, in business and in rugby. He was not a man who suffered fools or who entertained the idea that he was the fool.

Doc Luyt, Kitch Christie and Francois Pienaar were very close when I first started playing for Transvaal and Francois, in particular, was always seen as Doc Luyt's favourite rugby son. The trio made a potent leadership unit. I think Doc Luyt related to Francois' business ambitions, as well as the way he inspired and led his teams on the rugby field. I'll say it again: Francois was the best captain I experienced. Those early years with Transvaal in 1993–1996 were particularly insightful for me to learn from a proper rugby leader. Francois was a very good player and he could handle himself in any situation. He was physical, loved to tackle, didn't mind bleeding and took more than his fair share of head knocks. I also found him articulate and clever and he was a guy with edge because of a tough upbringing. Francois could scrap with the best of them but also sit around a business table with highly regarded professionals.

Doc Luyt and Francois were visionaries in how they saw rugby as a business and not exclusively a sport. Francois, in 1993, had been at the forefront of setting up the Transvaal Players' Trust, in which there would be team bonuses for every title won and the players' share in the bonus would be dependent on how many matches each one played. Doc Luyt was encouraged by Francois' ability to think out the box and I, as a young player, found it educational to learn from Francois as a leader. He also had a work ethic, be it in how to improve our environment as players or in how he trained and led from the front. He was a captain you could go to war with, and he was a captain who made young and old players think anything was possible.

What set him apart was that his evolving sophistication never became a mask for his roots. He never denied a past in which there was as much rogue as there would be revolutionary in his future.

I considered Francois a friend when our rugby careers finished and I still consider him a friend. I know how important he was to the success of Transvaal in 1993 and 1994 and, of course, the Springboks in the winning of the 1995 World Cup.

Francois' strength in motivation extended to negotiation and as a young player I was impressed by what he managed to negotiate on behalf of the players.

I trusted him and he was always transparent with us as players, as to what he was trying to do, whether it was the formation of the Transvaal Players Trust or in creating sponsorship opportunities. He would go sell our services as players and all he wanted to know was that we were committed to plans that were aimed at improving each player's financial situation. For example, if he needed a player to be at a golf day or to be at a function then it had to happen, and that player knew what was expected once there.

In those days, all I wanted was to play rugby, prove myself as the best in my position and enjoy my friendships, most of which were outside rugby. My Transvaal and Springbok teammate Japie Mulder and I had invested in a business in 1994 and if there was money to be made from playing, I wanted in. In the early 1990s, though, any money received from rugby was a bonus.

In 1995, pre-World Cup, the math was simple: I got my monthly retainer, my match fees and I hoped the team won trophies because that would translate into win bonuses through the Transvaal Players Trust.

What followed after the Springboks won the World Cup in 1995 changed the game forever and also changed the lives of all the players who were part of the Springbok World Cup campaign. My suspension from the tournament after the sending-off against Canada didn't mean I was excluded from any financial benefits of winning the tournament. The same applied to winger Pieter Hendriks, who was also suspended and banned from the World Cup after the Canadian match.

Both Pieter and I had left the squad once suspended and neither had any contact with the squad for the remainder of the tournament. It was a difficult time for both of us and we were resentful that we had been singled out after the Canada match and had our World Cup ended. You only have to watch the video footage of the fight that broke out to know that several players in both teams could also have been sitting at home.

Both of us had enjoyed such good matches in the win against the Wallabies at Newlands and we knew that we were the number one choice in our respective positions but we accepted that the rules of the tournament didn't allow for us to be near the squad after our suspensions.

I retreated for much of the tournament and stayed away from attending the quarter-final against Samoa in Johannesburg and the semi-final against France in Durban. I watched both matches in privacy and was thrilled we won but also angry not to be a part of the wins.

The country was engulfed in World Cup fever and I will always be grateful that as a player I did get to experience the emotion of the people of South Africa in the first three weeks of the tournament. The last three weeks were painful in that I felt such contrasting emotions in now having to be a spectator.

Did I want the Springboks to win? Of course I did. It got to me, though, that my understudy at Transvaal, Chris Rossouw, was the one who wore the No 2 jersey in the World Cup final. I didn't hold it against him personally; I would have felt the same regardless of who started as Springbok hooker.

It was such a strange space to be in because I was at the coalface at the start of the tournament and so distant from the action when it finished. I did watch the final at Ellis Park after I got an invite from some business people to be a guest at their private suite. The day is one I will never forget but how I would have loved to have been on that field!

Pieter and I would reunite with the squad the week after the tournament and the World Cup trophy would be paraded around the country as a thank you to the people of South Africa. It was in that week that I heard the talk of a professional breakaway rugby organisation. The name Kerry Packer was mentioned and, as players, we were told that it was going to be as life-changing as it would be game-changing. The players didn't think rugby was anywhere close to turning professional internationally in 1995. The game's administration was entrenched in amateur ways and any talk of player payment or professionalism was met with sour faces, even though every country was paying its best players some form of compensation to keep on playing provincially or internationally.

Some of the numbers being mentioned were outrageous and it didn't seem realistic. Just the year before, Japie and I had become partners in a chemical business but when we heard the amounts it was like winning the lotto, only no one had yet played SA's national lotto because no one was sure it actually existed.

Francois, as captain of the Springboks, was the primary negotiator on behalf of the World Cup players. He was the one interacting with Kerry Packer's representatives and he would be the one who had to deal with Doc Luyt when it came to the counter-offer from South African rugby.

I never questioned Francois' integrity in any discussions and was always comfortable that he would get us the best deal, if there was in fact a Springbok deal to be done with the breakaway organisation.

One week after the World Cup final, Francois shared the details of the Kerry Packer-backed offer with the 28 of us who had been involved in the World Cup, and before that we had been told that rugby in the southern hemisphere was about to conclude the biggest ever broadcasting deal in the history of the game with Rupert Murdoch's News Corporation.

Francois presented each of us with a breakaway organisation contract that included numbers. Clearly so much work had already been done between Francois and Packer's people. Personally, I was thrilled and when I saw the numbers I signed immediately.

Francois gave each of us all the detail and made it clear that the breakaway organisation could only become a reality if we, as a World Cup-winning squad, all signed. We had to be all-in as a collective and he said that Australia and New Zealand's squads had already signed.

It would now be a waiting game for us as players and we were instructed not to sign any other contracts that could legally counter our commitment to the Packer breakaway.

In Francois we trusted and then in Francois we'd have to trust again when all hell broke loose at Transvaal because the squad, as a collective, had requested increased salaries.

In 1993 and 1994, Transvaal were the best provincial team in the world and the core of that side contributed to South Africa's 1995 World Cup win. But even before the tournament there was agreement within the squad that we should be paid more.

The feeling among the Transvaal players post-World Cup was that the win had elevated our standing as players at Transvaal. We felt we deserved an increase in salary and that it was reasonable to demand a better retainer. We were world champions and wanted to be treated as world champions. Our individual reward for winning the World Cup was R100 000 which, after tax was closer to R60 000. There was, at that stage, to be no other reward.

Doc Luyt wasn't interested in entertaining our request and he let it be known that we wouldn't be getting anything different as Transvaal players - his only concession was a small increase in our match fees. Many of the more senior players were livid and they refused to accept the decision without a fight.

And a fight is what we got.

Training was cancelled on the Monday night and the players who had been the most vocal, among them Hennie le Roux, Rudolf Straeuli and Johan Roux, were fired the next morning, which led to Francois calling a crisis meeting at his place.

I knew I didn't want to be at war with Doc Luyt and that I wanted a long and healthy provincial career at Transvaal. Francois was the captain but I had led the U21s and been earmarked as a possible successor to Francois one day. I didn't want to jeopardise anything when it came to my rugby at Transvaal. I always got the feeling Doc Luyt liked me and was prepared to invest in me as a player and I also knew he supported how Kitch had included myself and Pieter after the World Cup.

I was initially reluctant to be part of the meeting as I felt it would be a betrayal of Doc Luyt and my employer, the Transvaal Rugby Union. Japie and I were at our business that morning when the drama of the player sackings started to unfold and I know he shared a similarly fearful view when it came to fighting Doc Luyt.

Francois was trying to save the situation and ensure we spoke in one voice but that morning I wasn't sure whether we should be speaking at all. Japie and I eventually agreed to attend the meeting and at the gathering, Francois told the squad that the most telling statement we could make was to stand together. Our requests were not unreasonable, we all loved playing for Transvaal. We had won titles and wanted to achieve more success.

Doc Luyt was a master of the 'divide and rule' policy and there was as much fear among the players as there was respect when it came to the man who paid our salaries. I felt he could target the likes of myself as a young player and that he had the means to alienate the younger players from the more seasoned squad members. He was an intimidating man.

Francois was concerned that Doc Luyt could get to the younger players and scupper any progress in the talks, which is why he was so emphatic that the only way we could be successful was to be united as a team. We all agreed to this but I, for one, didn't know what it would be like when confronting the immense business presence of Doc Luyt.

We decided as a group that until the situation was resolved we would not be training and Francois said he would inform the head coach Ray Mordt, as well as Doc Luyt of the team's decision.

Doc Luyt agreed to meet the squad on the Wednesday morning at his offices, and we all met at Francois' house the night before to prepare for the showdown. We all had to be on the same page but it was difficult because there were contrasting emotions about the possible consequence of our strike action. Some felt it had to be a confrontation or we would be doomed but I admit to being among those who felt we were going to be doomed because of the confrontation.

Doc Luyt's reputation was the stuff of legend at Ellis Park when it came to meetings and we knew all meetings were taped and that he was meticulous in dissecting a tape conversation and squashing the enemy. In this instance, he would have viewed the players who had delivered the treasured Currie Cup trophy for the first time since 1972 as the enemy.

None of us knew Doc Luyt better than Francois, which is why

he kept on preparing us for what was to come. He pleaded with us to stay focused, not speak unnecessarily and allow him to calmly present our position.

Naturally, Doc Luyt made us wait in the boardroom and this only played on our anxiety. Francois saw the tape-recording machine and asked me to check if it had a tape in it. It did and he instructed me to take the tape out, so that the meeting couldn't be taped.

Doc Luyt, on entering the room, told us the meeting would be recorded and asked if we had an objection. Even though we did, none of us had the courage to say so publicly and he wasn't amused when he discovered there would be no taped session because the tape was gone.

I was a mixture of nervous energy and fear because Doc Luyt had a way of talking anyone down and of making players feel very small, no matter their physical stature. It quickly became apparent that he hadn't agreed to a meeting with us to agree, but rather to insult us because he felt we had insulted him.

It was all a bit of a mind-fuck watching it unfold.

The discussion didn't get past our monthly retainer. Francois, on behalf of the team, said the players felt it should be increased, along with additional benefits. The number mentioned was an increase from R7500 to R15 000 per player, per month. Doc Luyt sniggered at any suggestion of an increase in retainer and thanked us for serving the union so well and wished us well in the future.

"How about I fire you all and buy a new rugby team?" he asked.

In that moment I literally shat myself, and I can say with some form of certainty that I wasn't the only one.

Doc Luyt's parting words, as he left the room, were along the lines of him finding players who would be more than happy to get our monthly retainers.

If we, as players, had walked into the room feeling united, in that moment we were everything but together. There were some who wanted to run, others who wanted to turn and some who were standing firm. I wanted to run!

The strike lasted the rest of the week and none of us were selected to play Eastern Province on the Saturday. Kitch Christie, his heart as much with Transvaal as it was with the Springboks, got involved to find a solution and between him and Francois, they got Doc Luyt to agree to considering our proposal. In return we all had to give a public apology (of sorts) for bringing the game into disrepute. I don't know if we ever quite managed to articulate the media response as Doc Luyt had instructed us to, but there was enough of a concession from us to the media for him to reinstate the fired players and to allow us to be selected for the next Currie Cup match.

We were all again officially employed but things were never the same between Francois and Doc Luyt, which was sad because in the negotiation, Francois had stayed true to all the leadership qualities that made him so successful on the rugby field. He fought for his players, which is what I believe Doc Luyt would have done had the roles been reversed. The damage wasn't restricted to Francois and Doc Luyt's relationship - the only common bond between Hennie le Roux and the president was that one played for Transvaal and the other ran Transvaal.

Things became strained and also weird in 1995.It should have been the most inspiring of seasons because of the World Cup win but it turned into a domestic hell for those Transvaal players who had been part of the tournament. There were so many distractions because of the possibility of most of the country's provincial players signing with Packer's breakaway league, there was the ongoing feud between Transvaal's World Cup Boks and Doc Luyt and there was also a Currie Cup campaign in which we would eventually fail to make the final.

Many of the players were struggling after the high of the World Cup, which in many ways is understandable. How do you go from winning the World Cup straight back into a domestic campaign? The more Transvaal struggled to put in commanding performances, the more the media let rip. We were accused of being on vacation and of being entitled, and we were mocked in the media for being a team capable of being the best on the planet but not the best in South Africa. When we lost to Western Province, the Cape media let us have it and wrote that we could win in the World Cup but not in the Currie Cup.

A once-off Test was played against Wales at Ellis Park, and even though we won easily enough, even that seemed to offer little joy in the context of what had unfolded after the World Cup. Personally, it was the biggest moment for me to be in the Springbok starting team and to be playing as world champions. It was my first Test back since the World Cup suspension and to be playing it at Ellis Park made it more memorable.

It was also the Test in which Kitch had so psyched up Kobus Wiese about the qualities of his opposite number, Derwyn Jones, that Kobus' response was to knock out the Welsh lock early in the game. It came at a lineout and dear old Derwyn was lights out. I am sure when he eventually woke up, he didn't know if he was in Cardiff or Johannesburg.

The upshot was Wales hardly won a lineout ball after that and Kobus comfortably enjoyed catching the darts that I sent his way. Kobus was fined R50 000 for the punch but Kitch, sensing that it may have been his pre-match baiting that had caused Kobus to lose it, paid the fine. Kitch, for all his meticulous planning and calm, wasn't afraid to whip the boys into an emotional frenzy, and in this Test, it ended the day for Jones.

The Packer breakaway uncertainty continued for a few months in the latter part of 1995 and, as a young player, all I wanted was certainty that something was going to happen where there would be greater financial reward.

Doc Luyt and the South African Rugby Union were determined

to keep the World Cup squad in SA and eventually the situation was settled at a meeting at his home, first with just the Transvaal Springboks and the next day with the entire squad.

Doc Luyt, with the financial backing of Rupert Murdoch's Newscorp, matched any offer we had signed with the Packer breakaway organisation. Francois, right until the end, acted with absolute transparency and integrity. He spelt out the gains of risking with the breakaway organisation but also highlighted the security we'd get by realigning with SARU and remaining based in South Africa. Each player had to make his own decision and whatever the majority, that would be the squad decision. History shows the majority decided on what could possibly be seen as the conservative choice, but at the time there was nothing conservative about the offer that had been matched.

The World Cup Springboks were all contracted to the South African Rugby Union for a three-year period and we went from earning R7500 a month to upwards of R150 000 a month. But we also knew there was nothing glorious about the inglorious way in which the truce had been agreed.

This was a resentful transaction that had been forced on Doc Luyt and the leadership in South African rugby and that resentment extended to the provincial players in the country who felt that they'd been betrayed because the majority of the World Cup squad had reneged on the Packer breakaway contract. It made for an ugly situation at a time when South African rugby should have been glowing.

The World Cup contract meant I could buy my first house, invest money into the business and spoil myself because I'd never been in such a financial position. All that was left in the year was to go to Twickenham and beat England in the final Test of the season.

The Springboks hadn't played England at the 1995 World Cup and there was a sense among the players that it was the one victory missing from the World Cup campaign. Australia, France and New Zealand had all been beaten and if we beat England on their home ground, then there could be no dispute as to us being the world champions.

We stumbled past Italy in Rome but there was never going to be a stumble in London. We were up for this match and the arrogance of the English players added to our motivation. England's South African born and schooled Mike Catt had been bullish in the media about England's chances. He also insulted Francois by questioning his ability as a rugby player, and his role as Springbok captain. It really got under our skins and it certainly got to Kitch, who reminded us every day of Catt's comments. Kitch was loyal to Francois and I, for one, was not going to leave Twickenham without letting Catt know how I felt about what he had said. As the week unfolded it became clear the entire team felt a sense of duty to sort out Catt.

It was my first Test start against England after being on the bench in the 1994 two-Test series in South Africa, but I knew what kind of physicality and gamesmanship to expect after being on the winning side when South Africa A and Transvaal beat them on the very same 1994 tour.

To beat England, you couldn't take a step back physically. To beat them at Twickenham you also had to arrive with more than just a physical presence. They weren't the most skilled side but they were hard men who thrived on physicality. We also enjoyed that aspect of the game but we couldn't be sucked into an arm wrestle when we had a backline with such attacking potency.

My memory of the game is that they were never in it because we never allowed them to settle. Another highlight was the first-half performance of Western Province front-ranker, Toks van der Linde. Kitch entrusted me with getting Toks into the right frame of mind, which meant getting him mad as hell and then letting him loose on the English. My pre-match pep talk focused on the Anglo-Boer war. I told Toks what the English had done to the mothers and children of his forefathers and that our only response was to smash them in a legalised game of rugby. The more I spoke, the more Toks grunted. I was happy he was ready to land a blow for every injustice of a war that quite frankly I knew very little about.

I'd always heard the Afrikaans guys talking about their hatred for England based on the war and tapped into that one line, and Toks responded with the most compelling of first-half performances, legal and illegal. Such was Toks' fury that Kitch called me over at half-time and told me I needed to stop winding him up and that he now needed to focus on playing rugby and not the history of the Anglo-Boer war.

We really played well that afternoon. Francois was brilliant in how he handled the pressure and how he channelled his aggression and energy, and it filtered through to all of us. Kitch's game plan was executed to perfection, especially his instruction that every early ball goes from the boot straight up onto Mike Catt, so that the former South African could experience first-hand the qualities of Francois Pienaar as a player and the support Francois had from every teammate.

Rarely has a rucking experience been so enjoyable and the only surprise at the end of the match was that Catt still had a number on his back. Kudos to Catt because he took his beating on the day and went on to have a celebrated career with England.

My first Test experience at Twickenham had turned into a treat but never would I have imagined that a first for me would also be the last in that I'd never again play in a Springbok team captained by Francois Pienaar and one coached by Kitch Christie.

1996 WINTER OF CONTENT

There was a moment when I wondered if I would ever get to play the All Blacks. I had warmed the bench on the Springboks tour to New Zealand in 1994, with coach Ian McIntosh preferring Natal's John Allan. In 1995 I was suspended when the Springboks won the World Cup final against them and in August of 1996, I again found myself on the bench in Durban for the first of the three-Test series against our greatest rivals.

Andre Markgraaff, appointed to the Bok job in 1996, was the third Springbok coach I'd play under in three years and, even though I went through the pre-match ritual and the high of finally fronting the men in black, I did not engage in a scrum, let alone a tackle.

John Allan was Mac's boy in 1994 and Markgraaff initially entrusted him to start in the Tri Nations, but it didn't yield different results as Allan didn't win against the All Blacks in three attempts during 1994, or two more in 1996.

Markgraaff favoured bigger hookers who he felt would give the scrum greater presence and strength. Throughout my career, however, I'd proved that a hooker doesn't have to weigh 110 kilograms to be effective. In the first 35 Test matches I played, we lost just three.

One of those defeats came in the second Test of the 1996 series in South Africa, when the All Blacks beat us 33-26 in the most dramatic of matches. I replaced Henry Tromp with 15 minutes to go and was convinced we could at least draw the match when we attacked ferociously in the final few minutes. The All Blacks had never won a Test series in South Africa and victory at Loftus Versfeld in Pretoria would be history-making for them.

Those final 15 minutes were frantic in that it was all-out South African attack. The crowd noise was incredible and it was as if 50 000 spectators, plus the 15 Boks on the field, were pushing for a final converted try that could keep the series alive.

The third and final Test was to be played at Ellis Park and, up until that point, the All Blacks had rarely won there in the history of this rivalry. They knew the significance of a ground that had a reputation for spooking them and the manner in which they defended their line at Loftus in those final minutes of the second Test was as much about making history in Pretoria as it was about knowing they'd be incapable of winning the series in Johannesburg.

They hung on, history was made and my 15 minutes against the All Blacks was not one of fame, but pain. It hurt to lose and it felt even worse because we had come so close. I wanted to be part of history against the All Blacks but this was the wrong kind of history. Fortunately, a few years later I would get to experience the right kind of history-making against them.

Playing off the bench at Loftus was my first time fronting All Blacks captain Sean Fitzpatrick and I loved testing myself against the player, who for the best part of a decade, had been regarded as the best hooker in Test rugby. He was also the All Blacks captain and individually it didn't get bigger for me than playing against him, with Ireland's Keith Wood the only hooker in my era who would rival Fitzpatrick's all-round game.

We lost but I had finally done enough to convince Markgraaff that a hooker with skills, doggedness, mongrel and attitude could do the job, even if he weighed less than 100 kilograms. My 1995

Rugby World Cup final against the All Blacks would come 14 months after the official one when I lined up to face the haka in the third Test of the series at Ellis Park.

The All Blacks picked their strongest side, despite having won the series, but I got a sense they were mentally already on a plane home. They were still tough but they lacked the desperation I had experienced from them in Pretoria and we had all the desperation after four successive defeats to them in 1996.

The highlight of my international career was always playing the All Blacks. They came with a reputation and with a presence that commands attention. They were like these black knights in armour and the power of the colour was almost invariably matched with the power of their performance. The haka was also thrilling to watch because I saw it as a challenge and an invite to go to battle. Some may view the haka as pre-match entertainment but I saw it as the start to the match. If you weren't switched on facing that haka, you'd never get the chance to switch on during the game. You'd take a beating.

I was proud to be a Springbok standing there and understanding the significance of the cultural war dance. You weren't just playing an opponent, you were playing legacy, history, culture and then the player.

Fitzpatrick will always be among the most iconic of All Blacks and it gives me great satisfaction when I think of the success that I had against him and the highs we had as a team against the All Blacks, starting with a dominant performance at Ellis Park in 1996.

We won 32-22 after leading 32-8 with only a few minutes to go and I started and finished the game.

The wait had been worth every one of those 465 minutes I warmed the bench against them and Fitzpatrick was as gracious in defeat as he was in your face on the field.

What I enjoyed about him the most as a player was that he

could give it and he could take it, whether it was a chirp, a punch or being cleaned out in a ruck. He was intelligent but he was also hard and in the times that I played him, we never held back when having a go at each other.

He was also so clever in getting an advantage at the scrum engage. For example, in 1996 and 1997 there was no distance in the scrum engage and it was first come, first set and first go. If you and your pack were ready, you went and the opposition ordinarily had to follow. If you set first it was a decided advantage, but what he would do so often is allow the opposition to set, then retreat and, as you hesitated, he'd move forward with his crotch over your head to mock a mistimed engagement which then forced the referee to pull up the opposing hooker. It was in that moment, as I was being pulled up by the referee, when he would then engage in tandem with his tighthead prop, who would be slightly in front of him. The two would then hit me at an angle, into the ribs and both would drive me upwards and milk a penalty, or at least plead to the referee for a penalty. None of it would be legal today but I am sure Fitzpatrick would have found a way to manipulate the scrum and referee if he was still playing.

Fitzpatrick was a great competitor and he knew how to work the referee. I used to call him a proper alley cat because he always seemed to get away with his shenanigans.

I confess to landing the odd big blow on him. Springboks and Sharks lock Mark Andrews reckons in the Durban Test match in 1998 he actually saw Fitzpatrick's lights go out from one of my punches but I wouldn't know because he just kept on playing, scrumming and getting from one set phase to another. His lights may have been out but his motor was still running. He was that kind of player.

I genuinely liked playing against him because he may have manipulated referees and pissed off the opposition, but he was never one to bitch and moan about getting hit. Fitzpatrick, like me, accepted that the cuts and bruises came packaged with the position. Both of us were masters of creating just enough of a gap when we engaged for our locks to land an uppercut on the impact of the engage. It really was old-school stuff but with today's cameras and television match official replays you don't find the dark arts being practiced too much. The game really has been cleaned up and when I watch some of the clips from the Springboks battling the All Blacks in the 1990s, many of those Tests in today's climate would have started 15-a-side and ended 7-a-side.

Fitzpatrick was as technical as he was hard. He was good at engaging late and at an angle, so that he could butt you on the top of your eyelid and cut you quickly.

He was generous in his praise after we beat the All Blacks at Ellis Park in 1996 and he was from the old school whose rugby students believed that what happened on the field, stayed on the field.

Markgraaff was elated after we won and I can't say he was humble in victory. He boasted that the Springboks should have won the series three-nil, which was taking it a stretch. I think the two teams were very evenly matched and the three-Test series was as close as the World Cup final and the first Tri-Nations Test in Christchurch in 1996. We won by three points in 1995, they won by four points in Christchurch, then by four points in Durban and a converted try in Pretoria. Our 10-point win seemed massive in the context of those results.

I savoured the win, even if the critics tried to downplay the significance of the result on the basis of the series having already been decided. As a player, there is no dead-rubber against the All Blacks and also no meaningless victory. It felt good to win against them in front of a capacity crowd of 63 000 at Ellis Park. The fortress had once again proven a graveyard for New Zealand.

I'll remind you of the All Blacks starting XV in that Test and it may make you appreciate why we took so much from the victory. It read, from 15 to 1: Christian Cullen, Jeff Wilson, Frank Bunce, Walter Little, Glen Osborne, Andrew Mehrtens, Justin Marshall, Zinzan Brooke, Josh Kronfeld, Michael Jones, Ian Jones, Robin Brooke, Olo Brown, Sean Fitzpatrick and Craig Dowd.

You had to have something about you as a team to beat that line-up.

A fire was starting to burn brightly within our squad after the three-Test series. Gary Teichmann had replaced Francois as captain and while I always felt Francois should have been leading the Springboks in 1996, I was very impressed with Teichmann as a captain. He was very different to Francois but no less committed and I considered myself fortunate to have played under both of them.

I didn't agree with Markgraaff's views on Francois and always believed he was intimidated by what Francois had achieved at the World Cup in 1995. The new coach and Francois had very strong personalities and Markgraaff wasn't prepared to play a secondary role to an established Springbok captain. I also got the impression that Markgraaff was insecure because of the relationship Francois had with Kitch and it was as if he viewed Francois as an extension of Kitch.

I could also never take seriously Markgraaff's claims that Francois faked an injury against the All Blacks in the 1996 final Tri Nations Test at Newlands in Cape Town. Francois was concussed and carried from the field on a stretcher but Markgraaff told the media that Francois had given up and didn't want to continue the Test. It was nonsense because the Boks were leading at the time, Francois and the rest of the Bok pack were dominant and in all my rugby-playing experience of Francois as a teammate at Rand Afrikaans University (now the University of Johannesburg), Transvaal and the Springboks, he simply never gave up. He was as tough as they come.

Transvaal's World Cup Springboks, who had formed the core of Kitch Christie's success, were on the outer with Markgraaff and, in the early part of 1996, the likes of myself and lock Kobus Wiese had to prove time and again that we deserved to be part of Markgraaff's plans.

Life was treating me well and I felt I was treating life well. I was focused on my rugby, had made a breakthrough to win back the starting hooker role under a new Bok coach and my business was blossoming.

I was settled and the happiest I had been in a long time, despite an awful start to the rugby year in the inaugural Super 12 competition. Transvaal's 1995 Currie Cup campaign had been a disaster because of all the sideshows with the Rugby World Cup contracts and while we got it together as players to hammer England at Twickenham at the end of 1995, the same intensity just wasn't there when we assembled for the first ever edition of Super Rugby.

Kitch was back with Transvaal and was going to split the roles as Super Rugby and Springbok coach, but he wasn't well due to a long-time battle with leukemia, and mentally so many of the Springboks were not in the strongest of places, myself included.

The summer had been one of revelry as we celebrated the 1995 World Cup success and the money we were now making. The mind and body just weren't in unison when Transvaal got back into training for Super Rugby in 1996 and we lost our first four matches in Australia and New Zealand.

The media crucified us, Doc Luyt refused to accept our performance and the strength of the 1993 and 1994 Transvaal team, which was unity, was a memory. The Transvaal squad of 1996 may have been similar in player identity but it was very different in attitude.

Kitch struggled because he was sick and Ray Mordt, as his assistant, was in a catch-22 of trying to be the boss but not officially being the boss. Doc Luyt's presence on our overseas tour also didn't ease tensions and we all felt the full wrath of his displeasure, especially when we lost to the Waratahs in Sydney. He kept us in the change room for a while and it was clear that the love affair of 1994 between the paymaster and his puppets was finished. We were now a team at odds with each other and very much at odds with our boss.

Kitch's illness meant he was replaced when we got back from tour, and with Ray entrusted with the head coaching role, we showed some improvement but not enough to ever be in a position to make the play-offs. We won just three of 11 matches, with one of those wins coming at Ellis Park against eventual champions, the Auckland Blues. That result showed we could still play but one big game in the tournament wasn't enough to convince the new Bok coach Andre Markgraaff that Transvaal's 1995 World Cup-winning players should be at the heart of the home series against the All Blacks.

Markgraaff, as I have mentioned, did soften with the likes of myself and Kobus Wiese, and we did reward the Bok coach with our performances against the All Blacks in the final two Test matches of 1996 in South Africa. We also showed enough in the Currie Cup to be selected to tour Argentina, France and Wales at the end of the year.

Argentina and France were each two-Test series while Wales was a one-off Test in Cardiff which was also the last time the Boks ever played at the old Arms Park.

Markgraaff was in his element after the Ellis Park result against the All Blacks and he was a different man on the end-of-year tour because he was no longer threatened by the Francois Pienaar factor and he seemed more secure in the team environment. He was very vocal about his working relationship with Teichmann as his captain.

Look, Markgraaff is no Kitch Christie and the two shouldn't

even be mentioned in the same breath but my loyalty has always been to the jersey I was wearing and when I played for the Springboks, my support and commitment was to whomever was coaching, whether the coach and I liked each other or not.

I was fortunate to experience one year of Bok rugby with Kitch as my coach and it remains my most special because of how much I rated, respected and liked him. But I also enjoyed the way Markgraaff integrated himself into the players' environment.

Kitch was specific about the familiarity between him as the coach and us as his players: there wasn't any. Kitch was a good man and a father-type figure, whereas Markgraaff was a good oke and more like one's China.

Markgraaff loved the familiarity and he wanted in on everything. He loved to talk to everyone about everyone and anything. He saw a conspiracy theory at every turn and if there wasn't one, he'd be the conspiracy. He trusted no one and felt the world was out to get him, but he had a passion for the Springboks and for South African rugby.

I felt I could talk to him easily and I could even share a joke with him. With Kitch I was "Bullet", but with Markies' he would always affectionately bellow "Dalton" before barking out commands. I think there was an element within Markgraaff's psyche that still wanted to be a player, as much as he was a coach, and there was most definitely the desire to be the president, as well.

I found him an interesting combination of personality and a colourful character and once I had shown him that I was capable of doing the job as his starting hooker, he showed me loyalty in never making me doubt my position. He picked me to start in his last five Tests in charge, two of which included the first series-win by a team in France in a decade.

I was living life to the fullest at the end of 1996. Business was good, my friendships were strong, my soul brother Camillo was sharing my house with me, I was single and enjoying the simplicity of being in that space and I had won over the Bok coach through performance.

Little did I know in December that within the first eight months of the next year I'd have to prove myself to the fourth and fifth Springbok coaches in the space of four years, and that I would be falling hopelessly in love. Early in the summer of 1996 I would never have imagined the roller-coaster ride that would take me to the apex of my international rugby career and plunge my life into chaotic free fall.

LURED ONTO THE DARK SIDE

Carel du Plessis is an amazing man and the best wing to ever play for the Springboks. He was a remarkable rugby player but he had no clue about coaching an international team and he had no coaching experience at all. As a person, he was softly spoken and very gentle in his communication. You couldn't but like him and if you ever watched him play the game, you couldn't but be awed. I had so much respect for Du Plessis the rugby player but as a coach he was a joke. At the end, it was a battle divorcing the respect I had for his rugby-playing with the lack of respect I had for him as a Springbok coach.

Try as I did to understand his ways, I just couldn't. And I know I wasn't alone.

Carel did things as a player very few would have been able to. He did them naturally and with such ease, but he found it difficult to articulate the most basic aspects of the game to the players. His assistant coach was Gert Smal, another of those men who had made such an impact as a player but never quite reached similar heights as a coach. Gert would coach the Stormers and be Jake White's assistant coach when the Springboks won the 2007 World Cup. He would also coach Ireland's forwards and he clearly improved with more experience but in 1997 I found him one-dimensional and schooled in an archaic and outdated approach to training. He was very uninspiring as a coach.

Gert and Carel had been close as teammates and were close friends but the duo, as a Test coaching combination, were out of their depth in 1997 when the British and Irish Lions toured South Africa. It remains among many inexplicable decisions that the duo was ever appointed to succeed Andre Markgraaff, who had resigned in early 1997 because of accusations of racism. Markgraaff had used offensive and abusive language towards a black South African Rugby Union administrator when talking to a provincial player at Griqualand West. The player taped the discussion and released it to the media when Markgraaff, who was heavily involved with Griquas as a provincial union, failed to guarantee the player a contract extension.

I admired the way Markgraaff handled the situation because he didn't deny anything. He took accountability, called a media conference and explained the context to what he said, why he said it and to whom it was said. He then resigned, knowing the scandal was too big to save him as the Springbok coach.

I watched his media conference and felt sorry for him as he wept. I knew the feeling of addressing the country at a media conference and being reduced to tears because the emotion was overwhelming. It had happened to me after my suspension from the 1995 Rugby World Cup. I know Markgraaff wasn't everyone's kind of person, but I didn't find him offensive and I thought he had a unique charm in a strange kind of way. I had grown to understand him on the 1996 end-of-season tour to Europe and, from a rugby perspective, I thought he and Gary Teichmann had formed a strong partnership as coach and captain. Markgraaff, perhaps because of Gary's personality, didn't feel threatened. Gary is a strong character but he was very comfortable in giving Markgraaff the security that the coach was in charge. The Springboks returned to South Africa at the end of 1996 with good reason to be optimistic of winning the home series against the British and Irish Lions.

Then it all went to pieces after the drama of the Markgraaff tape scandal.

There was uncertainty among the players as to who would succeed Markgraaff, and when Carel was announced there was even more angst because of his lack of coaching experience. Would the new coach consider Super Rugby form and the performances of the Boks on the European tour, or would he want to clean out for the sake of cleaning out?

Once again, I found myself questioning where I stood in the pecking order. I'd never worked with Carel and Gert as a coaching combination and my experience of coaches in South Africa was one of provincialism and pre-determined judgement. I didn't know whether I would even get a chance to meet them in person so they could judge me on how they experienced me as a rugby player, and I questioned whether the media prejudice against me would derail any potential national call-up.

The media in South Africa, especially in Gauteng, always felt I was lamp-post material on a Monday morning when it came to my life outside rugby. I did not conform to the stereotypical Springbok rugby player, especially because I had a very sound business, was not obsessed with rugby and remained loyal to my friendships outside the sport, many of which were linked to the nightclub scene in Johannesburg and unconventional professions, like debt-collecting and protection.

Everyone always seemed to have a story to tell about me and the media especially would react to the story regardless of the accuracy of the information. It was something that started in the early 1990s and remains prevalent today.

One of the more absurd media stories, sold to the readers as an exclusive, followed my breakup with Caryn-Lee, a girlfriend in 1994 and 1995. We were living together and owned marmoset monkeys. They are very expensive and are popular to breed because of the financial spin-offs but our interest was in having them as pets.

Following our breakup, her mother went to the media with all sorts of accusations about me and said I wouldn't hand over the monkeys. The media lapped it up and mocked me about the monkeys and sought to humiliate me with monkey jokes. The only reason her mother wanted the monkeys was for breeding purposes and I refused to allow it. The reason I broke up with Caryn-Lee was that she had slept with another man in our bed at my house while I was on tour.

It crushed me when my domestic worker told me that another man had been sleeping over while I was overseas playing rugby. I am very secure in my profession as a businessman and was always confident in my ability as a rugby player because what I got from the game depended on what I put into training and match day. I could dictate my own result because it was directly down to me, but in relationships it was very different because different personalities determine the end result.

I consider myself vulnerable and insecure in relationships, which is why I have been single for such lengthy periods of my adulthood. The uncertainty, complexities and potential for hurt meant I found it easier to stay away from love in a partner than to seek it out.

My family upbringing was as brutal emotionally as it was beautiful on other levels. My father adored me as a son but he never showed my mother the same kind of love and affection and it influenced the way I viewed relationships. My sister is blood and because of that I will always have her back but she is no buddy of mine. We never had a relationship growing up and we don't have one now. I don't deny her existence and I've often helped her and her family but if she wasn't family, she wouldn't be in my life.

My childhood was a product of a complex family dynamic, in

which both parents loved me and gave me everything I needed but they never gave me the contented feeling that we were a happy family unit. It played on my conscious and subconscious and it has affected my relationships with partners.

The breakup with Caryn-Lee was difficult because I felt humiliation and shame that she had slept with another man. It also played with my ego and my reaction was one of self-preservation. The only way I knew how to protect myself was to stay away from girlfriend relationships.

That changed in 1997 with Shelley. She was the first love of my life and I was besotted with her. I'd do anything for her and I wanted to treat her in the most caring and loving way. She was undoubtedly my number one and I wanted, as much as I needed, to be her number one. In 1997 she was a secure pillar for me, and I felt I understood love in a relationship for the first time and knew I was experiencing it. My heart ached for her when I was on tours or away and, with her in my life, I felt settled and secure, which helped me deal with the uncertainty of team selection under Carel and Gert.

Transvaal's Super Rugby campaign had fallen apart after showing so much promise. The 1996 season was a shocker with three wins in 11, but 1997 started brilliantly and we won the first four matches, lost in the last minute to a penalty against the Hurricanes and then drew against Northern Transvaal. We were favourites for a semi-final but would lose all four matches on tour in New Zealand and Australia to finish the season in fifth place.

Transvaal's poor finish only complicated matters and my worst fears were realised when the Bok squad was announced for the one-off Test against Tonga at Newlands. It was more of a practice run for the three-Test series against the British and Irish Lions and my participation was limited to the last 30 minutes in a one-sided 74-10 win. There was nothing to be gained from the result and the match was a glorified contact session in the guise of a Test match.

Tonga were hopeless and there was no way of making a statement in that Test but the next month proved to be as frustrating for me as the 1994 Test series in New Zealand had been because I again found myself warming the bench. What made it even more unbearable was that I was benched for Naka Drotske, which I took as an insult.

The great and successful coaches are also very good selectors and in the early Tests I didn't think Carel got his selections right, with the exception of Percy Montgomery. Carel picked Monty at outside centre against the Lions and in the Tri Nations. It proved an attacking masterstroke, even if fullback proved to be the position in which Monty would excel in his Test career. Monty went on to kick the Springboks to a World Cup title in 2007 and became the first to ever play 100 Tests for the Springboks.

Monty was just a kid when he came into the Bok set-up and he formed an instant connection with the more experienced James Small. The two had played together at Western Province earlier in the season and in many ways, 1997 was the year in which James, the glamour boy of the Bok backs, passed on the baton to his successor. Both James and Monty were like moths to a light when it came to media attention. They were the pretty boys and poster boys of Springbok rugby, and, on the field, they were lethal on attack. I liked both of them as people and continued to enjoy a friendship with each of them long after retirement, even though Monty and James drifted apart in the latter part of Monty's international career. I once asked James why he didn't stay in touch with Monty and his response was that their lives had taken different paths; James felt his time had passed and that it was now Monty's time.

As a rugby lover I have to thank Carel for doing Springbok rugby a service and picking Monty in 1997, but for me, that was the only significant coaching contribution of Carel's very brief stint.

We lost the first two Tests against the Lions in Cape Town and Durban and I felt powerless sitting on the bench. It was New Zealand 1994 all over again and, as I said previously, there is no more empty feeling than being on the bench in a Test match and never getting to play.

With the series lost I finally got my chance in the third and final Test at Ellis Park, and it reminded me of the final Test during the previous year's series against the All Blacks. The atmosphere was similar, the opposition seemed to have one foot on the plane and we were psyched. Ellis Park, as a venue, inspires the Boks as much as it intimidates the opposition. We smashed the Lions and I felt I had made my case to be the starting hooker in the Tri Nations.

Carel and Gert didn't agree and my personal experience of the tournament was one of extreme emotional contrasts, with South Africa suffering a then record 55-35 defeat against the All Blacks in Auckland and a fortnight later crushing the Wallabies 61-22 at Loftus Versfeld in Pretoria.

I started two of the four matches but for me it wasn't good enough and the inconsistency in our performances was also not good enough. There were so many fantastic players in the Springbok squad that there could be no justification for winning just two of the seven matches against the Lions, Australia and New Zealand.

Those supporting the appointment of Carel and Gert would have felt vindicated by the way we dismantled the Wallabies but I've never seen an Australian team give up like they did in the last 20 minutes in Pretoria. It was as if they were playing to get rid of their coach and our record win had as much to do with our destructive attack as it did their mental disintegration. They just didn't seem to care.

It is always good to end a tournament in the starting XV and even better when the result is with a record score but as I was finding out every year, it was no barometer when it came to Test selection because you never knew whether the same coach was going to be there the next time the Boks played.

Provincial rugby was waiting for me after the euphoria of the Wallabies victory and, as with the Boks, Transvaal's coaching structure would see Kitch retire in 1996, Ray Mordt come and go and former All Blacks coach Grizz Wyllie entertain us with his war stories and antics more than any coaching desire.

Grizz was a giant in New Zealand rugby folklore, both as an All Blacks player and as an All Blacks coach but by the time he made his way to Transvaal, via Eastern Province, he was more interested in drinking than developing a world-class team. He was a character but he was from a rugby era that had passed and he refused to accept the game had passed him by. Unfortunately, I learned nothing from Grizz and the players looked at him with amusement, even though I am sure they would have found him amazing in his glory days.

Shelley made coming home from tours a pleasure and I liked being with her. We celebrated each other and the relationship was very passionate. We really loved being together but, while she had eased my insecurities, my growing friendship with Peter Conway and Rob Reynolds only increased her insecurity.

I'd met Conway and Reynolds through my good friends Julio and Carlo, who had a working and social relationship with my oldest and dearest friend, Camillo. Julio and Carlo did enforcer work for the Hells Angels, and were partners with Camillo as debt collectors.

Conway and Reynolds became the face of the Johannesburg-based Hells Angels in the late 1990s and later, an elite extension known as the Nomads. They ran the show when it came to the exclusive supply of ecstasy drugs to the Johannesburg nightclub owners. The trade-off was simple: no one else supplies ecstasy tablets and in return, the nightclub owners get guaranteed protection and security services.

I knew of Conway and Reynolds in the early 1990s. Our paths crossed at various times but there was no real bond between us until the late 1990s, with 1997 the start of the friendship.

Conway and Reynolds were big players in the underworld and this had always intrigued me. It excited me on some level and allowed for an escape from all the discipline that was synonymous with my upbringing and sporting career. My father is a disciplinarian and to be successful in rugby I had to be disciplined, and mostly I surrounded myself with those who would influence my need to be disciplined to succeed in my rugby.

Carlo and Julio played in a different world and Camillo has always had the common sense and grounding to understand the role he wanted between both worlds. All three were very clear about who they were and what they did and all three were equally clear about the fact I was a Springbok rugby player with a great sporting future. They never did anything to derail my career and we would hang out because of friendship, in spite of the different worlds we inhabited. I didn't want to get involved in their world and none of them wanted to be a Springbok rugby player.

Conway, in particular, was different. He liked being feared because of his reputation. He also liked the fact that he could hang with a Springbok rugby player and his narcissism played into every insecurity in my ego when it came to wanting to be liked and loved in relationships. You could say we fed off each other, but for all the wrong reasons. I was attracted to the fact that his world was so different to the one I operated in on a daily basis, be it running my business, that of a professional rugby player representing his country, or just a guy in a normal and settled relationship.

Shelley warned me about Conway and she saw the ugliness in our friendship. She had experienced problems with Conway before I had ever met her. She had spoken of an incident between the two of them and told me that he scared her and that he was capable of terrible things. I told her she had no reason to be scared: he was my mate and that she had to accept he was in my life as a friend.

I had an amazing, beautiful romance with this incredible woman and as much as I was blinded by love, I was also blinded by the illusion of who Conway was and the world in which he lived.

You watch movies as a youngster and the bad boy is always the hero. It is the one you want to be but the romance of a moving ending isn't how it plays out in real life.

Conway, as our friendship strengthened, had a hold over me and so did his world. I considered myself a leader and not a follower but when it came to Conway, I followed. I tried to make sense of it and have often spoken to Camillo about it. His view is that Conway's world was the opposite of everything I knew and, in Conway's world, I didn't have to be a leader and take responsibility, I could be anonymous and just be one of the pack.

There is truth to Camillo's observation because I felt free hanging out with Conway and Reynolds, I felt untouchable and I felt I owed no one anything in that world, be it by way of a rugby result, an individual performance or in a business sense. When I played for the Boks, the eyes of the country's people were on me but with these guys, the only eyes watching you were the ones they wanted to glance their way.

It gave me a distorted sense of being and power, even if there was no premeditated intent to want to abuse this power. I had always toed the line when it came to authority, from my father to my teachers and rugby coaches, but there was nothing restrictive about the authority I felt when I was with Conway and Reynolds. There was a reckless disregard and freedom that, whatever the action, there wouldn't be consequence.

I was being lured into a world that was unprotected but it *felt* protected. Deep down I knew it was wrong, dark and bad and it pains me to say it but at the time, it excited me. Most youngsters aspire to be the Bill Gates of the world or a CEO of a company and here I was, a Springbok rugby player, successful in my own right, wanting to hang around with gangsters and criminals. I don't know what that says or said about me as a person but I found comfort in being with these guys.

It was alluring and I was engrossed, and for the first time ever I started to struggle to separate the two worlds. Conway was no longer just someone who I hung around with in nightclubs or at the Hells Angels quarters. He was now a mate who visited my house regularly and he was among those closest mates who would want to be in the stadium when I played for South Africa.

The closer Conway and I got, the further apart Shelley wanted to be. I just wouldn't acknowledge the situation and the repeated warnings. I should have removed myself but instead of listening to her, I kept this devil in my life and entered a really fucked up world.

MALLETT: A PLAYER'S COACH

Nick Mallett stood larger than life as he welcomed us as his first group of Springboks in 1997. He had a definite edge about him. He had toured with Andre Markgraaff's 1996 Springboks as an assistant coach and was very popular with the players. He was knowledgeable and if you may have doubted him in any way, he'd be the first to remind you that you could doubt many things in life but to doubt Mallett was simply stupid.

He was bullish in the way he spoke and brash, but his prose was also powerful in how he articulated his views on the game, on the players and especially the opposition.

I had found Carel to be timid and half apologetic when he addressed the players and he lacked gravitas standing in front of us as the Springbok coach. Mallett was the opposite and he seemed to have grown even bigger with his promotion from assistant coach in 1996 to head coach a year later.

He loved to speak of himself in the third person, but hell he was a character. He could tell stories, he called it like he saw it and I've never known a coach who could so comfortably tell the English-speaking players that they were picked to think and the Afrikaans-speaking players that they were there to tackle. He also struck an immediate rapport with Gary Teichmann and they had a bond very similar to Kitch Christie and Francois Pienaar. They were also opposite in personality and character but that added to the potency of the partnership.

Not only did they like each other, but there was obvious respect between the two as coach and captain, and that kind of thing filters through the squad very quickly. Gary was well liked as a captain and he comfortably rose above the provincial bias that existed among players. It didn't matter which province you were from, you took to Gary as a person - as a player and as a leader. He was understated, which complemented Mallett, who was very stated in his words and his actions.

The leadership of Mallett and Teichmann immediately instilled confidence in the players and I had only ever experienced a similar comfort with the 1995 Springboks under Kitch and Francois.

What I liked about Mallett was his honesty in any interaction and from the outset you knew exactly where you stood as a person and as a player. He didn't try to be a friend if he didn't relate to your personality but he would still pick you first if he thought you were the best player to start the Test.

The biggest downfall with coaches is when they try and play mind games and play two players off against each other. It invariably backfires because players talk to each other and they talk among themselves. The happiest and most successful teams I was involved in during my career were born because of the coach's conviction in identifying his first-, second- and third-choice player in every position.

Mallett told me from the outset on our 1997 tour to Italy, France, England and Scotland that I was his number one hooker and, as a player, that was manna from heaven. I responded to this kind of communication from a coach, and if he had told me that I was second choice, I would have had as much respect because I know he would have given me the reason why and then let me know what I needed to do to change his opinion.

Western Province had won the Currie Cup under Harry Viljoen and they had played the type of rugby that made Harry's 1991 and 1992 Transvaal teams so exciting to watch. Mallett had picked the core of the Province backs, which included James Small who had played in Harry's early Transvaal teams before moving to the Sharks.

Mallett was clever in selecting so strongly from the Western Province backs, but the Currie Cup final didn't lull him into dismissing the claims of other very good players from across the country. He was very astute in his selections, which was a tribute to his instinct and appreciation of what he looked for in a player, specific to a position and combination. You didn't necessarily agree with him and he frankly didn't care, but if you questioned his selections, he'd have an explanation as to why and if he didn't rate a player, he would simply tell him so.

We all knew Mallett had played for the Western Province team that won five successive Currie Cups and that he had played in France and coached there for more than 10 years but I never saw him as a Western Province man because he never treated one provincial group of players any differently to the other and he didn't have the coaching history to be accused of such bias.

Ian McIntosh, having coached Natal all his life, invested heavily in his provincial players and Kitch's first instinct was to look to the players he knew from coaching Transvaal. Mallett was a unifier of provinces in his selection. The Test team that produced that stunning performance against France at the Parc de Princes didn't include one of the Western Province Currie Cup-winning forwards, but he started key WP backs in Percy Montgomery, inside centre Dick Muir and wingers Pieter Rossouw and James Small. Mallett's selection of the pack was a coaching masterstroke, and it showed in the results.

Over the years, I've heard many people say that Carel should have been given more time as Bok coach and that Mallett inherited his team that humiliated Australia in Pretoria. As a player who was in the squad, I don't think Carel should ever have been in the job and Mallett should have been in the job earlier.

Mallett also didn't just take that team from the Wallabies Test and head to Europe. He was strategic in the changes he made and, because of positional switches and new selections, the starting line-ups between the Tests in Pretoria and Paris were radically different. Monty went from outside centre to fullback, Andre Snyman from left wing to his preferred position of outside centre, Pieter Rossouw was picked at left wing, Henry Honiball was restored to the No 10 jersey (having worn No 12 against Australia), Dick Muir was at inside centre and Werner Swanepoel added a different component at scrumhalf in the absence of the injured Joost van der Westhuizen. In the forwards, the changes were also telling because Mallett added the iron man Andre Venter to a loose-trio of Rassie Erasmus and Teichmann, while introducing the very good Northern Transvaal lock Krynauw Otto and Sharks tighthead prop Adrian Garvey. This team was at the heart of the unbeaten five-Test tour in which we demolished Italy 62-31 in Bologna, repelled a French comeback to win 36-32 in Lyon and sealed a second successive Springbok series-win in France with a stunning 52-10 display in Paris. We never let up after the high of Paris and, as the best teams do, we backed up one great performance with another and then another, whipping England 29-11 at Twickenham before embarrassing Scotland 68-10 at Murrayfield.

We were the hottest rugby property in Europe and the United Kingdom in November and December 1997 and Mallett was a revelation as coach. He charmed the international media as easily as he chastised them and he could romance and ridicule the opposition without changing his expression.

Mallett, in 1997, was the ultimate players' coach. His communication was clear and there was never any antagonism between player and coach because there was never the elephant in the room when it came to selection. He didn't bullshit any player and if you were number one in your position you knew it, the guy who was number two knew it and the entire team knew where they stood in terms of selection.

Mallett also trusted and entrusted the senior players like Teichmann, Dick Muir, Mark Andrews, Henry Honiball, James Small and myself, but promoted a youthful balance with his selections. I knew I was his number one and in turn he expected me to play like I was his number one. He never questioned my status as his first-choice hooker and I backed that up with performance and attitude. I left everything out there for him on that tour and I was no different to every other player given an opportunity.

Any win at Twickenham against England is special and in the 1995 and 1997 victories, Joost van der Westhuizen and Andre Snyman scored two of the great individual tries. But the most memorable match of the tour, and one of the Test highlights in my career, was the rugby we played in putting 52 points past France in Paris.

It was spectacular and when it was over the French crowd rose in appreciation of the champagne rugby we had played. I don't think I have ever seen Mallett that happy because his Springboks had played the near perfect game of rugby in a city that was his home for nearly a decade. Nick was fluent in French, had coached Stade Francais to two successive Top 14 titles and was seen by the locals to be as much a Frenchman as he was the coach of the Springboks.

Our celebration afterwards was equally impressive at the James Joyce Irish pub, opposite our plush five-star Concorde Lafayette Hotel. Mallett always encouraged us to mix with South African supporters and to embrace the media. He tried to educate us that it could only be to our benefit to have a good relationship with the media and that many an issue could be settled over a drink, as opposed to in the press. The travelling South African media on that tour celebrated with as much relish as every player and person in the Bok management. It was the most enjoyable Springbok rugby tour I would ever experience and I finally felt as though we were playing like a national South African team, united in one cause, as opposed to a team of South Africans safeguarding and protecting their provincial affiliation. My props Os du Randt and Adrian Garvey were from different provinces, locks Mark Andrews and Krynauw Otto played for the Sharks and Bulls and the loose-trio was a combination of Sharks (in Teichmann) and Cheetahs in Erasmus and Venter. The halfbacks were a Cheetahs/Sharks pairing, the midfield WP and Sharks and the back three WP, with Small having played for Transvaal and Natal. It was a coming together of South African provincial rugby in the name of the Springboks. Mallett, in his selections, had shown it was possible and we as players had responded to his faith in our ability.

The veteran South African rugby writer, Gavin Rich was a favourite among my generation of players and he drank merrily with us at the James Joyce on that famous night in Paris. He described the evening as the most raucous and enjoyable post-match celebration ever with the Boks, and his recollection of the night also recorded Mallett's masterfully delivered speech that the coach made to the players and management. Mallett, as Gavin would recall in his book on Springboks coaches, said: "Guys, whatever happens with this team, whatever we may or may not go on to achieve, I can tell you that we will always look back on this day with special affection. If any two of us happen to run into each other in 20 or 25 years' time, no matter where we will be or what we are doing then, we will be able to look back on this match and, suddenly, there will be a very powerful bond between us. We have shared something very important today. You must all enjoy it."

Enjoy it we most certainly did and, in that moment, I had no reason to doubt that it was a performance that would forever bond those players whose rugby skill and talent had combined to produce such ball-in-hand poetry.

We had conquered Europe and the United Kingdom and a rugby season that started so sweetly with four successive Transvaal Super Rugby wins had ended spectacularly.

ENJOYING THE LIMELIGHT

I was King of the Castle when I got back from the overseas tour at the end of 1997. I felt untouchable and behaved as if I was royalty, had my own principality and could do what I liked. I had played well on the tour, enjoyed five successive Test match wins and was at the peak of my rugby powers. I just needed Nick Mallett to stay on as Springbok coach because each time I had come back from a winning end-of-year tour for South Africa, I'd awake one morning in the New Year to read that the Bok coach was fired or had resigned.

I knew that 1998 was going to be a big year in South African rugby because for the first time, our teams would be playing as regions, not provinces, but I feared the worst when it was decided to merge the Johannesburg-based Lions with the Bloemfontein-based Cheetahs. The two teams were historically bitter rivals and each was very proud of its own identity. The Lions had always been Transvaal and the Cheetahs were always known in the Currie Cup as Free State.

Now we'd be playing as the Cats and, supposedly, playing in the name of a united franchise representing the region and also South Africa. Geographically it made no sense whatsoever, given the distance between Johannesburg and Bloemfontein. Culturally, the players from the two regions are polar opposites and generally the players would have very little in common. There would be a few of us who knew each other because we played for the Springboks and I'd become close with Rassie Erasmus and Werner Swanepoel during the end-of-year tours. I really enjoyed them as people and rated them highly as rugby players.

Rassie and Smiley (as Werner was known) would make being in Bloemfontein a bit more bearable, but I am a *boytjie* from Johannesburg and I loved playing for the Lions and living there. I had already experienced Bloemfontein in my first year out of school and I just couldn't fit in. I found the pace too slow and the lifestyle from another century. I needed bright lights and activity, and I needed to be around my friends. Knowing they were just up the road, gave me a sense of security. I've always needed an escape from rugby and my life has never been consumed by rugby. I would give everything in training and playing but once the game was over I didn't want to be near rugby players and talk about rugby. In Bloemfontein, the only big lights were at the Free State Rugby Stadium. Thinking about going back to Bloemfontein made me feel claustrophobic.

The Cats' players would be based in both Johannesburg and Bloemfontein and our home games would be split between Ellis Park and the Free State Stadium. Oom Peet Kleynhans and Gysie Pienaar, the revered Springbok fullback of the 1980s, coached the Cats in their debut season.

I was anxious about both the Super Rugby season and being away from my girlfriend Shelley for extended periods. The four-week tour to Australia and New Zealand was emotionally taxing and my experience was that the South African players took strain on those tours, especially in the last two weeks. The Kiwi and Aussie teams would only have to travel to South Africa for two weeks and those additional two weeks away were influential in the league standings. It was one thing to be away with the Boks and your own province but to effectively be away when we should have been at home was a challenge that I struggled to beat.

The thought of having to be in Bloemfontein for extended time gave me a sinking feeling, so before I had to face that pain, I treated myself to a bit of time in Cape Town with my best mates Camillo, Julio and Carlo, and boy oh boy did we have the best of festive seasons!

It wasn't always pretty, it was on occasion messy, but hell I loved it. I never judged Carlo and Julio on how they made their living and made their money. It wasn't for me to judge or to care. What mattered was the bond we shared as friends. Camillo was similar in that the only person he judged was himself and if he was content with his day then it was a good day. I took those early lessons from Camillo but when it came to my personal relationship, it wasn't quite as simple.

I'd started to befriend Peter Conway and Rob Reynolds in 1997 and Julio, Carlo and Camillo knew them well. Julio and Carlo did a lot of enforcer work for Peter and Rob privately and on behalf of the Hells Angels when Conway and Reynolds took over running the biker gang.

Julio and Carlo were dangerous men professionally but socially, in friendships, they were the most loving of mates and the most caring. They could come across as gentle giants if you didn't know them but if someone crossed the line in an insulting way, they'd pay the price and it was never pretty to witness.

Julio and Carlo were a lot closer to me than Peter ever was and we experienced a different kind of friendship. Julio and Carlo knew when it was work and when it was play, just like I knew when it was rugby and when it was play. For Peter, the lines were always blurred, even though in 1998 and 1999 I couldn't make sense of just how blurred they were.

For two years I benefitted from the 1995 World Cup contract I signed with the South African Rugby Union but I knew the lotto money would be finished in the last few months of 1998. Going into that year, I appreciated how well I'd have to play to make the Springboks and justify being paid the highest category in the new contracting structure.

I was in love with Shelley like I had never been with any woman, had played the best rugby of my career and was seeing some amazing financial numbers in my chemical business. I felt I owed myself a release and a gift, so I decided to buy a Harley Davidson while we were in Cape Town. I couldn't ride a motorbike and had never had an interest in bikes but if you want to even be considered for the Hells Angels, then you have to be over 21 and own a motorbike with an engine capacity bigger than 750cc.

I woke up one morning in our Camps Bay hotel during the summer break at the end of 1997 and told Julio we needed to find the Harley Davidson shop in town because I was going to get a bike. He didn't blink, even though he knew biking had never been my thing. Within a few hours, I'd contacted my mom, who was dealing with my accounts and asked her to make a transfer of R200 000. That afternoon I was the owner of a Harley Davidson, although you could say Julio must have felt he was the owner because he was the one who had to ride it. I was more than happy to be the passenger.

We did some stupid things in Cape Town that summer and we also did some civil things, and the stupidity cost us money. I felt happy and strong. I had wasted cash but I felt I deserved to be reckless, even if only for a couple of weeks.

My childhood was never about having excess money and we as a family were disciplined with money. Even when I got my first payment from the 1995 World Cup contracts, I took responsibility for the privilege. I invested in property and the chemical business and while some may say a Harley Davidson is an investment, there was a small voice in me that knew it was an indulgence. It spoke more to my ego and need to be acknowledged by Conway than it did to any obvious interest in having a Harley Davidson.

When I look back it is so obvious which path I was going

down because when I first met Conway and Reynolds, I was very particular about what I enjoyed and why I hung with them. Then, I could easily divorce the two worlds but now I found myself wanting in on their world more and more.

It wasn't the cleverest move because it also took away from my mystique to them. I was the first-choice Springbok hooker and that was the identity I should have kept, because they had such a high regard for Bok rugby players. When I told them I wanted to be a prospect, with the potential of being patched and made a full member of the Hells Angels, I gave Conway all the power in our relationship.

I may have thought I was in control of everything because rugby gave me a sense that it was business as usual but I was lying to myself. My relationship with Shelley was starting to suffer and so was my chemical business, both of which I would never be able to fix because when I did come to terms with what was going on, it was all too late.

Conway and Reynolds never took advantage of my desire to want to be a Hells Angel and they never treated me like any of the other prospects that hung around their headquarters, which bizarrely was called 'The Church'. We certainly weren't doing any religious worshipping. It was quite the opposite.

I'd officially be there at least once a week when I was in Johannesburg and not away with rugby and Camillo and I would hang out there a lot. I can't recall us ever having to pay for a drink or anything else that was on offer, and there was an unwritten respect paid towards the two of us. Camillo had no interest in being patched and, if you will excuse the pun, he came along for the ride. Free drinks, free drugs and free women.

But I was being seduced into the gangster world you see in movies and naively thought it was one I could play in because I had this belief that when it got too intense and uncomfortable, I would always have my rugby world.

I was wrong.

The deeper I got in, and the more I connected with Conway, the worse the plunge seemed to be. I was struggling to find a way back into those disciplines that had always made me good at rugby.

It wasn't like I hadn't been warned.

Shelley, oh, Shelley, why didn't I listen to you? It remains my greatest regret.

I am so sorry for us; for you and for me. I really am.

I had it all with a woman, whose character and beauty was everything I could desire, and I fucked it up.

My behaviour in the early part of 1998 was out of sync with anything anyone had known from me. I was distracted and not focused and, not content with the expense of a Harley Davidson, I even bought a Ducati when I still couldn't ride a motorbike. I'd get on the bike, start it, rev the engine and then play passenger while one of my mates took control. Bikes were not me and one of the funniest stories is me actually going to motorbike school to learn how to ride a 'big boy' bike and then finally ride my Harley Davidson and Ducati. The romance of big bikes was nothing like the reality of me owning a big bike. I thought I was going to be schooled in the art of riding Harleys and Ducatis but, when I got to the motorbike riding school, I was put on a 125cc and I hardly managed that. It made for a hilarious afternoon and I accepted that I shouldn't give up my day job as a professional rugby player and business owner.

I was able to laugh at myself when it came to me and motorbikes but I was finding in 1998 that I wasn't laughing too much about life. I was not in a good place, even though I couldn't see it, or didn't want to see it.

Shelley warned and cautioned and exhausted herself warning and cautioning me about Conway but I refused to see what was in front of me. I was hanging out with him more than I was with her and he was at my place way too often for her to ever feel comfortable. She didn't keep quiet about her distaste for what she was seeing. Peter would come round, we would talk shit, drink and then we'd leave. Sometimes, I'd only get back the next morning.

There was respite from the madness when I was out of Johannesburg but I was playing for a new franchise with no identity and no soul. The prospect of the international season was my sporting motivation and, fortunately, Nick Mallett was still the Springbok coach.

Playing for South Africa in 1998 would restore my sanity and force me away from the darker world which had begun to consume me. At least, that is what I was telling myself.

The Cats concept never worked, not in 1998 and not in any year the franchise existed. Laurie Mains, in 2000 and 2001, would take the Cats to the semi-finals of Super Rugby, but he did so by primarily selecting a team from the Lions players he coached in the Currie Cup, and when the Cats played those two semi-finals away from Ellis Park, they were easily beaten.

Oom Peet Kleynhans, head coach of the Cats in 1998, was out of his depth but he was also on a hiding to nothing when it came to players. If he picked too many Lions, then he would have been branded a sell-out by the Free State players, and the same was true for the Lions players if too many Free State players were in the starting line-up. I think he tried to balance selections according to where we played our home games. If at Ellis Park, then more Lions players. The same principle applied for the Free State players when playing in Bloemfontein. Why would locals come to watch Lions players in another jersey and accept these players as their own? It was another thing if you were wearing the Springbok green and gold at any ground in the country but franchise rugby was a foreign concept to a South African audience who had only known provincialism for the past century.

For all the indifference around regionalism and the lack of unity within the squad, we won our first match of the 1998 season against the Bulls and were the following week leading the defending champion Auckland Blues with a few minutes to go. The Blues, like the All Blacks in my time, always seemed to be spooked when coming to Ellis Park. It was the venue where Transvaal won the 1993 Super 10 final against Auckland, the Boks won the 1995 World Cup final against the All Blacks (and beat them in 1996) and where the 1996 Lions beat Auckland, despite only winning three matches that year.

The Blues had won Super Rugby in 1996 and 1997 and were a very settled combination under Graham Henry, who would go on to win the World Cup with the All Blacks in 2011. In 1998, they had heaps of All Blacks in the starting XV but the Cats matched them minute for minute and try for try until the final moments. Blues fullback Adrian Cashmore knocked over a simple conversion on full-time to end any fairy-tale start to the history of the Cats. We lost 38-37 and that was about as close as it would get for the Cats in 1998. We'd lose every match before ending the season with a meaningless win against a severely depleted Stormers team that was then still called the Western Stormers. The Cats, in everything, were shambolic but the Western Stormers were an even bigger mess. I remember speaking to James Small afterwards and he couldn't stop cursing when it came to how the season had unfolded for them. It had started with Harry (Viljoen) as coach and ended with assistant coach Alan Solomons taking over. Harry and James were very close from the time when Harry coached Transvaal (1991-1992) and the Sharks (1993), and Harry had inspired James' move from the Sharks to Western Province in 1997 where they won the Currie Cup. Province were outstanding in 1997 but the 1998 Western Stormers were awful. They were also struggling with regionalism and there was pressure to select players from South

Western Districts and Boland, to appease the administration in those regions. Western Province were the primary feeder to the Western Stormers, yet some of their players were missing out in the name of regionalism. The Sharks were the exception because they played as a region but their coaching staff selected the team as if it was a Sharks provincial line-up. The region comprised Eastern Province, Border and the Sharks. I think all they did was financially compensate the two smaller unions, change the jersey to a different type of black, play the odd match in Port Elizabeth and East London and call themselves the Coastal Sharks. But, in essence they were the Sharks Currie Cup team, which also explained why back then they were the only team to have a measure of success in Super Rugby.

The performances of the Western Stormers, Bulls and Cats were diabolical and the trio propped up the log, but there was always going to be enough quality within the South African player pool for Mallett to pick a very strong squad for the two-Test series against Ireland and the one-off Tests against Wales and England.

Mallett had told us at the end of the 1997 tour that he would be loyal to the players who had made such an impression against Italy, France, England and Scotland. If we were fit and in reasonable form, we'd get a call-up and once in camp we'd be able to take it up a notch.

When I look back on my career, it never got better for me than those weeks when we dazzled the rugby world with our brand of Springbok rugby and started our march towards equalling New Zealand's then world record of 17 successive Test wins.

We started the season against Ireland, confident of adding two more wins to our winning sequence of six, and we were sure that number would be 10 by the time Wales and England had returned home from South Africa.

I didn't rate the home unions very highly at the time and didn't see them giving us anything more than a contact hit out before the Tri Nations. What I couldn't have imagined was that the Irish series would turn into a cage fight.

I was psyched to be playing Ireland because it would be the first time that I'd oppose Keith Wood, who was regarded as the best hooker in the northern hemisphere and in the top three in the world alongside myself and Argentina's Federico Mendez. New Zealand's iconic captain Sean Fitzpatrick had suffered a knee injury in 1997 that would bring his Test career to an end. Fitzpatrick had set the standard internationally in his 92 Tests and with him gone, myself and Wood now had a two-Test series to put down a marker as to who was number one.

South African-born Dion O'Cuinneagain would make his debut in Bloemfontein for an Irish side coached by New Zealander Warren Gatland. Mallet emphasised to the players that Gatland's approach would be based on physicality and he would bring a typical New Zealand edge to the Test match. The Irish would also have an advantage because of O'Cuinneagain's knowledge of South African rugby and insights into several of our players. O'Cuinneagain, who was schooled in the Western Cape, had played for Western Province and the Springbok Sevens and was well liked by those Springboks who knew him. He was considered a good oke and we certainly weren't going to underestimate the challenge of Ireland.

We knew they would be robust and we recognised they had some world-class individuals but we didn't think they had the overall quality to beat us.

Mallett, true to his word, stuck largely with the side that had finished 1997 with a 10-try 68-10 win against Scotland at Murrayfield. The only change in the pack was Ollie le Roux at loosehead because Os du Randt was unavailable. The backs were rejigged with the fit-again Pieter Muller at inside centre and Joost van der Westhuizen at scrumhalf. Mallett would also start the Test with Gaffie du Toit at flyhalf in the absence of Henry

Honiball and Jannie de Beer. The pack was our strength and it had become very settled during the end-of-year tour. It was also a pack that would become more potent during the Tri Nations.

Gary Teichmann was now entrenched as the captain and he was a very popular choice among the players. I really enjoyed Teichmann's approach because he believed that every player was the captain of his respective position and he allowed each player to take responsibility and lead himself. Gary knew when to step in and pull us together, but he wasn't the type of captain who relied on hysteria or Braveheart-type speeches to work us into a frenzy. He was very calm, which allowed for Mallett's extroverted and animated personality to thrive. Springbok rugby had something very good going with Nick Mallett and Gary Teichmann as the leadership in 1998.

The Bloemfontein Test was a bittersweet one for me because Mallett had chosen Stefan Terblanche at right wing, which was a selection that would end James Small's international career. James had been a permanent fixture on the right wing for South Africa since the first Test back in international rugby in 1992, and the two of us had shared many a great moment on the field and off it during our international careers in 1995, 1996 and 1997. James had scored two tries against Scotland at the end of 1997 to claim the record for most tries scored in Bok history. He would not have thought that would be his last time in the Springbok jersey, and not having him in Bloemfontein was a reminder to me that it didn't matter who you were and what you had achieved, there was no guarantee you'd be there the next weekend.

James' axing was the bitter part of the Test and the sweet belonged to Stefan who was outstanding in scoring four tries on his debut. Stefan was totally different to James in character but he was similar in the attacking impact he would have for South Africa.

We won 37-13 in Bloemfontein and were never troubled. We prepared well for the match and I expected more from Ireland in terms of physicality and rugby pedigree. Wood was a tough competitor and I enjoyed the individual challenge. He would try and hurt you by running into you, and as physical as he was with ball in hand, he had quite a mean streak by getting to your ribs from the blindside or "accidentally" rucking you. He gave it but, unlike Fitzpatrick, I found that he was very vocal when he got it back. He didn't like it, whereas Fitzpatrick accepted that if he threw a punch, one could be coming back his way.

Wood and I played a similar type of game because we both liked to carry the ball and hit it up into contact. We both wanted to be involved in the game and in the thick of things. We went at each other and there was plenty of niggle but he was the exception in their side when it came to world-class players, and it must have been frustrating for him.

What pissed us off in Bloemfontein was Wood swinging a haymaker punch at Gary. It was a punch thrown from the side, with Gary unsighted and unable to defend himself and it was the incident that would set the tone for the second Test in Pretoria. When I think of all the forwards I played with, Teichmann is among the most disciplined. He didn't throw cheap punches and he didn't instigate brawls. He rarely threw a punch. He was physical and could handle himself in any situation but he was a classy player who relied on his rugby intellect and skill to beat the opposition. He was also our captain and Ireland had obviously targeted him off the ball to evoke a reaction. It had come a little too late for them in Bloemfontein but they had said enough to us on the field for us to know it wasn't going to stop in Pretoria. They were going to keep on trying to hit Gary off the ball because they felt that if they could get him to lose focus, it would have a knock-on effect on the rest of us. It wasn't the brightest of approaches from the Irish.

The attack on Teichmann near the end of the match ensured there would be no socialising with the Irish afterwards. We kept to ourselves and had no interest in having a beer with their players. I think those Bok players who knew O'Cuinneagain may have chatted to him and congratulated him on his debut, but there was nothing hospitable in the way we acted towards Ireland and what happened on the field spilled over into the build-up to the second Test.

Mallett was typically critical of our performance but accepted it was our first Test of the year. He was a coach who celebrated each Test win and he encouraged the players to always enjoy every winning moment in a Springbok jersey but he was insistent about wanting a more clinical display in Pretoria. He also made it clear to all the players that no Springbok team allows the opposition to attack the captain and that we needed to let that be known very early in the second Test.

The scene had already been set for what would infamously be dubbed "The Battle of Pretoria". On that particular Saturday night in Bloemfontein, another battle had already played out in the car park of our hotel, and it concerned my mates Peter Conway and Rob Reynolds, who had driven from Johannesburg to Bloemfontein to watch the Test.

Conway loved being in my Bok world as much as I was starting to love being in his world and I'd given him and Reynolds a key to my hotel room. We'd arranged to meet there when I got back from the match and had finished with all the team post-match responsibilities.

Sometime in between the match finishing and our team court session, Mallett sought me out to let me know there had been a complaint from the hotel management that "mates of mine had fucked up some guys in the parking lot". He wasn't happy and had already made a judgement. He lectured me on what it meant to be a Springbok and said as much as I had a responsibility to the Boks, so did my mates. He spoke to me as if I had been the one beating up guys in the parking lot. It really pissed me off because he didn't ask me what it was about but assumed I knew what it was about.

I got to my room and Conway and Reynolds were there and in full voice, charged up and drinking. When I walked in Conway had my Springbok blazer in his hands and I flipped because no one touched my blazer. I told him to put it down and said that him picking up my blazer was the equal of me walking around with his Hells Angels colours and path in my hands. He understood my anger and apologised for showing me disrespect when it came to my Springbok blazer. I then told him there had been a complaint about a fight in the parking lot and his response was that a few locals had insulted him and Rob when they returned from the Test match. The locals had mocked the way Conway and Reynolds were dressed, in these biker outfits, and they had sought the confrontation without knowing who they were. Conway said the locals were belittling and the consequence was that these locals took a severe beating. He said the issue had been resolved and that there would be no police involved and that that locals had accepted the situation once they'd been educated as to who they had insulted.

Obviously, they hadn't fully accepted anything because they'd complained to the hotel manager, who had taken the story to Nick. These guys had threatened to take the story to the media and this is what Nick told me he wanted to avoid but what was there to avoid? No one from the team was involved and why should I be accountable for what my mates did after the Test match?

I went back to see Nick and said the story wasn't as one-sided as had been explained to the hotel manager. I told him what my mates had said and told him there were three versions to the story, which was Conway's, that of the locals and the truth. I again challenged what it actually had to do with the team and with me?

Mallett said the team didn't need that kind of attention in the media and that I had to make my friends aware of the damage they could do to me and the team, but it annoyed me that I was condemned when I wasn't even there. It was consistent with so much I'd experienced in my life where an immediate judgement would be made, without checking the facts and it always felt like I was apologising for things I hadn't done or for people's behaviour because I happened to know them.

I appreciated Nick had come to me but I didn't like being lectured for something I hadn't done.

Conway and Reynolds were in even better spirits when I returned to the room and by then I had calmed down. We'd beaten Ireland, I was content I'd got one over Wood and I finally felt I could let off some steam. Fuck it, I was with my mates and the night in Bloemfontein was going to belong to us, which it did, without incident I must add.

The media in the week played on the Wood cheap shot on Teichmann and the South African media climbed into the Irish for trying to target Gary. Nick had fuelled the media to put the heat on Wood. He was quoted as saying Wood should have been sent off and that the only thing that saved Teich was that the punch hit the back of Rassie Erasmus' head on the way to Gary's head.

Wood had apologised to Teichmann after the Test and he had also apologised in the media. He said it was out of character and in the heat of the moment, which I'd agree with. Wood wasn't a dirty player. He'd headbutt you and not stand back in a punch-up, but he wasn't the type to take aim at a defenceless player. I put it down to frustration and just knowing he was playing in a shit team that had no chance of winning.

Ireland's coach Warren Gatland refused to accept his players had done anything wrong and he told the media that his players were frustrated at how we slowed the ball down, slowed the game down and did it all illegally.

The papers that week made for entertaining reading and as players we knew the second Test was starting to boil over even before the first whistle. If players tell you they don't read the newspapers or internet or social media they're lying. Players read everything and some react to what they read better than others.

Our training sessions in Pretoria had an edge to them and there was increased intensity, which had nothing to do with a fear of losing to Ireland but more with Mallett being adamant that the Irish needed to be taught a lesson for taking to Teichmann in such a cowardly fashion.

Gatland had told the media that he had instructed his players that if the referee was not prepared to sort out our supposed illegality and slowing down of the ball, then his players would do it themselves. He was quoted as saying: "We will deal with it in our way" and we had been told that the word from within the Irish camp was that if a Springbok player was on the ground then he was going to be kicked. This fired up Mallett and with Mallett fired up, we were fired up.

If the Irish felt they could target Teichmann, then the obvious target for us was their talisman and best player Keith Wood. What unfolded was brutal and neither side's players held anything back. War had been declared in the week and it wasn't a rugby war.

From the first contact, there was off-the-ball punching and kicking. Both teams were guilty because neither team's players were willing to back down. We knew there was no way Ireland could beat us and we never doubted that we'd beat them, which we did 33-0.

It was an awful game of rugby, even though we scored five tries, had two disallowed and probably could have got another two. I scored one of the tries but my most memorable moment was putting in a legal and telling hit on Wood, getting in over the ball, letting him know what I thought of him and halting the move. It was one of the most satisfying collisions in a one-on-

one situation I had experienced in Test rugby. Wood had all the momentum, was flying and I met him head on, halted him as if he had hit a brick wall and put him to ground. If you think that's an exaggeration, check out the YouTube clip because it's there in a four and a half-minute package under the heading 'Springboks versus Ireland Battle of Pretoria'.

My tackle on Wood resulted in Ireland's replacement flank Trevor Brennan flying in with a haymaker, from which one of many brawls started. Ireland No 8 Victor Costello had attempted to clean me out off the ball and kneed me in the back. When I got up to follow him, he tried to collar me around the neck. I flipped him, pounced on him, pinned him down and landed four successive punches within a restricted space and with players on my back trying to pull us apart. His only defence was to get his fingers in my eyes and gouge me.

In today's sanitised world of rugby, we both would have been given red cards and we'd have been two of about five or six players on each side sent for early showers.

Wood would have gone for his off-the-ball shenanigans, Ireland's captain Paddy Johns threw enough punches and initiated enough cheap shots to have been sent off several times, and he didn't even get a caution after trading blows with Krynauw Otto and Rassie Erasmus.

Johns was out of control and what complicated the lawlessness of the match was that French referee Joel Dume let everything go, or he may have just decided the only way to deal with it was by letting the two teams punch themselves out. Whenever he blew his whistle to try and end a fight, another broke out.

The Irish, no match for us on a rugby field, were playing for their pride as men, and I could understand the mindset. If they weren't going to win the game, then they wanted to be able to say they won the fight. It's debatable whether they did. They'll feel they landed their share of punches but we handed out as many as we got.

The difference was we could still fight and play rugby, whereas all they had in them was anger. We dominated them in the collisions and they couldn't handle the physicality of our rugby or the skill set of our players. They were the ones slowing the game down and they offered nothing in the way of rugby from the moment Paddy Johns took a swing at Teichmann at an early lineout.

Johns should have walked and so too should Joost van der Westhuizen for his kick on Irish lock Malcolm O'Kelly. There can never be justification when a player kicks another in the head and it would make me a hypocrite to even try and defend Joost, who in today's rugby climate would have served a lengthy ban for his kick on O'Kelly. Johns would also have been in the stands for most of the year for the punches and for the way he cleaned Teichmann out in the ribs.

It was an ugly Test match and the nastiest of my international career but it was also satisfying. Ireland got nought and not only had we convincingly claimed the series two-nil, I'd also won my battle with Wood. In that moment, on that night, I considered myself the best hooker in world rugby.

DEALING WITH DISTRACTION

It was without doubt the worst Welsh team ever to tour South Africa and possibly the worst Welsh team in the history of the game. I even felt sorry for those players who had been picked to play us at Loftus Versfeld. No player asks to be selected and I guess no player turns down the chance to represent his country but I am sure most of those Welsh players would have figured that this was one tour to miss and that reputations could only have been enhanced through absence. I didn't know it at the time but a few years later I'd also get to experience that hollow feeling of playing Test rugby when you know your teammates just aren't good enough to be wearing the national jersey.

The Springboks won 96-13 and I remember the Welsh coach being asked afterwards where it went wrong for his team. His answer made me laugh out loud at the time and still today I laugh when I think about it. His sharp retort to the question was: "When they kicked-off."

I started against Wales and was among the many tryscorers but I'd played in tougher schools matches when I was at Jeppe. You couldn't even call this match a contact session, let alone a Test match. Test match rugby is supposed to be a test of one country's best against another's best, but in Pretoria on the 27th June in 1998 it was a case of South Africa's finest against Wales' worst.

We should have scored 100 points but Naka Drotske, who had replaced me in the 67th minute, dropped the ball with no one to beat and the try line 30 metres away. I don't know what the other players were thinking at the time, but I know I was pretty glad Naka spilled the pass because a rugby nation as proud as Wales should never concede 100 points in a match.

It's really pleasing to see how Wales have improved in the last decade under Warren Gatland and going into the 2019 Rugby World Cup in Japan they'd beaten South Africa in three of their last four matches, which was very different to how things were in 1998 when Wales had yet to beat the Springboks. I am a keen student of the game and every time we'd play Wales there would be talk of the vintage Welsh teams of the 1970s and of those Welsh players who were at the heart of the British and Irish Lions series wins against the All Blacks in 1971 and against South Africa in 1974. Unfortunately, my only recollection of playing Wales was that it was always a guaranteed win, even when I played in a very poor Springbok team in 2002.

In 1998, there was nothing poor about the Springboks and we were easily the best team in the world. Poor, hapless Wales will concur that they ran into a green machine that was oiled and fully operative.

I remember watching the carnage from the reserves bench in the last 10 minutes and Wales had used every substitute except one player. I looked at this poor oke and wondered if he was relieved or insulted that he still hadn't got on. The score at that stage was somewhere close to 80 and when we scored again, I just couldn't resist. I called to him and said: "Hey China, how shit must you be that they still won't put you on." I can't remember who he was but he did get on in the final couple of minutes and all he did was take up a position behind the posts when we scored our final try. I doubt he would ever have played for Wales again and I wonder what story he tells his grandchildren about the day he played for Wales against the Springboks at Loftus Versfeld. Somehow, I doubt it's the one I have just told you.

The win against Wales was our ninth in succession and now everyone was starting to talk about the potency of the Springboks and people were starting to speculate about how many matches we could go unbeaten, with two Tests against the All Blacks looming. South Africa's Tri Nations record in 1996 and 1997 was poor against the All Blacks in that the Boks hadn't won a game. Andre Markgraaff's 1996 team lost in Christchurch and at Newlands in Cape Town, and Carel du Plessis' team lost at Ellis Park and at Eden Park in Auckland. I didn't play in the 35-32 defeat against New Zealand at Ellis Park in 1997 but was in the front row when we conceded 55 points at Eden Park. We had led early through a converted try but All Blacks captain Sean Fitzpatrick, on his home ground, was at his masterful best in controlling the referee and also in getting under our skins. He had saved New Zealand from defeat against us in the final Test at Eden Park in 1994 when he milked a penalty from Brendan Venter. It was a Fitzpatrick special in how he got into a position to obstruct Brendan, then tugged at his jersey off the ball and ensured he was in the line of the referee when Brendan lashed out at him. Penalty New Zealand, and they'd equalize 18-all with the last kick of the Test.

Three years later and it was again Fitzpatrick the master manipulator at play. Admittedly, we would never have won the Test but Fitzpatrick was once more the antagonist and when Andre Venter retaliated, he got shown a yellow card. To play the All Blacks in New Zealand with 15 men is the toughest assignment in rugby and to play them at Eden Park, their fortress, with 14 men is an impossibility. They humiliated us and at one stage led 55-21 before we got some respectability with two late tries.

It was an embarrassing result and it was the first time a Springbok team had taken 50 points from the All Blacks. Even more embarrassing was reading in the New Zealand newspapers the next day what our coach Carel du Plessis had to say afterwards. He was asked whether it was the darkest day in Springbok rugby's history and he said no. He spoke about the positives and the bounce of the ball and the yellow card, and when I'd finished reading what he'd said it was clear he hadn't watched the same match that I had played in the day before. He spoke about scoring 35 points against the All Blacks and asked the media to recall how many teams had managed to do that against them in New Zealand. What he didn't seem to take into account was that they had scored 55 points against us in the process of conceding 35. It was a 20-points differential, and in those days that was a hiding of note.

A year later and the rugby landscape had changed significantly. The Springboks were on a roll and New Zealand had been criticised for how they'd played in Europe at the end of 1997. Mallett, typically, was bullish about our prospects in the 1998 Tri Nations because of the continuity in selection and because we were starting to develop a winning habit. The French series win at the end of 1997 had been huge for our confidence and we were starting to believe we could beat anyone, including the All Blacks.

We still had to play England in Cape Town to complete our June and July four-Test programme and we knew they would be cannon fodder. As with Wales, they'd sent a largely second-rate squad to tour Australia and New Zealand and they were preparing to finish their season with a one-off Test at Newlands.

Australia had whipped them 76-0 and they were also clobbered in the two Tests against the All Blacks. There was no way they could beat us.

Mallett knew it and the Bok players knew it.

Mallett wanted us to enjoy every success and Saturday nights were always cause for celebration, with Sunday being a flush-out day and Monday the start of the business week. I had been very disciplined throughout June because I was in camp with the Springboks. Peter Conway and Rob Reynolds had come to Bloemfontein to watch the first Test in the second week of June but I hadn't seen much of them since then. My relationship with Shelley was not good and it wasn't getting any better while I was away with the Springboks.

I was starting to feel the effects of my love life going south and the more I focused on the Tests, the more I longed for the intensity Shelley and I had when we first met, and for the normality of our relationship before I had invited Peter and Rob into my life.

I'd been with the Boks all of June and while I had seen Shelley when we were in Johannesburg preparing to play Ireland and Wales, it wasn't the same as being at home. I knew my relationship was in trouble but didn't think it was on the scale of the trouble the Welsh team had found themselves in when they played us at Loftus Versfeld.

The week in Cape Town would give me a week to try and clear my head because I'd be at home for a fortnight before leaving for Australia and New Zealand for the away matches in the Tri Nations. My rugby friendships were different to those friendships in my social circle. Camillo, Julio and Carlo knew me the best and former World Champion boxer Brian Mitchell is someone who will always be a friend. Brian and I had shared a place at one stage in the early 1990s and we were always in each other's lives in some capacity but in 1998 I'd hang with Camillo, Julio and Carlo and, much to the disgust of Shelley, you could add Peter Conway to that inner circle.

I didn't easily share my emotions or talk to anyone about my relationship with Shelley, but Camillo always knew what was going on in my life and I didn't have to talk to him for him to know something was wrong.

The Test against England in Cape Town provided a distraction to the real issue in my life, which was saving my relationship with Shelley. We won 18-0 in the most horrendous of conditions at Newlands and it said everything about the quality of our side that we could score 18 points in that weather. Nick, usually conservative with any praise straight after a Test match, was very complimentary that we were able to get a couple of tries and keep England scoreless. The conditions proved to be a leveller but there was no disputing the difference in class between the two teams.

The Springboks were now unbeaten in 10 Tests and the media were starting to talk about us having the players to go past the 1995 World Cup-winning team's 15 successive wins. Usually I'd be on top of the world after such a month of international rugby but I returned home fearing the worst and I got the worst. Shelley broke up with me. She told me she just couldn't cope with my friendship with Peter Conway and the evil she saw in our friendship. She said she didn't know me from the man she had fallen in love with and she didn't like what she was seeing. We had been through so much in a year and she had fallen pregnant and had a miscarriage. We were both distraught because we both wanted to be parents and I don't know if either of us recovered from the loss of our child. Shelley was a strong woman but she had also been through a lot when I met her. I had always found myself attracted to women with broken wings and I would take great care in wanting to fix them and be a father figure to them. I wanted them to feel secure and safe with me and know that I would look after them. I don't know if it is a projection and that the one with the broken wings is in fact me but with Shelley it felt different because I never doubted that I was number one in her life. I knew she would never be unfaithful to me, betray me or humiliate me, as had happened in my only serious relationship in the early 1990s.

It is what made the end of our relationship even harder - she didn't break it off because she didn't love me, or had found some other guy, she ended it because I refused to end my friendship with Peter Conway and it was this ongoing friendship that was destroying Shelley and myself.

I didn't know how to respond and I didn't have the emotional maturity to deal with the situation and neither did I have the desire to cut Conway out of my life. I was crushed to lose Shelley but refused to choose her above a lifestyle. With the likes of Conway and Reynolds, that was only ever going to end badly.

I felt pushed into a corner and believed I was the victim because if I had to think anything else it would have forced me to be truthful about the situation. Springbok rugby, my passion, was starting to become an escape and I wasn't confronting the real issues in my life. I looked to rugby to forget the mess of my private life but it was not sustainable because I could only think about rugby for so many hours in a day, and when I didn't think about rugby, all I could think about was Shelley.

So why didn't I simply cut off Conway and his world? You could ask the same question of a junkie who chooses drugs over love. I just couldn't reach the point that I didn't want to be around Conway, Reynolds and the Hells Angels, and I felt myself drawn more and more towards the chaos of Conway and his ways.

Conway, when I was with him, masked everything and he numbed whatever demons he was battling with booze, drugs, fighting and working women. I found myself in a similar situation and my father intervened. He told me to get away from Conway, Reynolds and the Hells Angels. He said Conway wasn't everything it seemed and that the word within Police circles was that Conway was a police informer and a snitch and that the Hells Angels was a front for him. My dad, a policeman all his life, told me Conway was a rubbish and not to be trusted.

I love my dad and consider myself particularly close to him. I trust he always had, and will have, my best interests at heart and I can only imagine what it must have felt like for him to feel powerless when it came to my friendship with Conway. My dad was not a man to ever fight my battles but even then, when he did step in, I couldn't recognise the situation and I found myself offended that he didn't trust me to make good decisions.

Conway and Reynolds were my friends and I refused to apologise to anyone, including my dad, for this friendship. I had already chosen the potential of being a Hells Angel and the poison of the friendship with Conway ahead of the love of my life Shelley and, in hindsight, the resistance to my dad's intervention was a clear indication that I already knew I had made the wrong life choices.

The tour to Australia and New Zealand couldn't come quickly enough. I just wanted to get out of South Africa, away from the lure of the Angels and Conway and away from the hurt and pain of losing Shelley.

The tour, I was convinced, would demand my full attention. I wouldn't have time to think about Shelley and I'd train myself into exhaustion so that when there was downtime, I'd be too tired to have the capacity to think or feel anything.

The reality is I was emotionally at a low and depressed.

I put on a front when I was with the team and was jovial and the eternal optimist. I continued to play the role of the tough guy at the back of the team bus and nothing in my on-field performance would have hinted at anything being wrong in my life.

I didn't speak to teammates about my situation and I would never have spoken to Mallett or any of the management because I didn't want them to think that this emotional turmoil within me would have a negative bearing on my rugby.

The Springboks were playing Australia in Perth, which by then was as much an away game for the Wallabies as it was for the Springboks, and even the Australian media were writing us up as favourites. We had gone 10 Tests without defeat and our performance in Europe at the end of 1997 was a talking point from the moment we arrived in Perth.

The Australian media enjoyed Mallett because he was so different to his predecessors, especially Markgraaff and Du Plessis, and his ability to engage with the Australian media meant we got very good press in the build-up to the match. There was a lot of respect for Mallett and for what he had done since taking over and there was recognition that we were the form team in world rugby.

The Springboks have always been talked up in Australia for our physicality but here the rugby reporters were writing about our skills and ability to score tries as much as we could scrum and maul.

It made for good reading and perhaps we all started believing our own press because we'd play our worst Test since Mallett had taken over from Carel du Plessis. Australia had a new coach in Rod Macqueen, who would lead the Wallabies to World Cup success in 1999, but on that night in Perth I would never have picked Australia to be world champions a year later.

We won 14-13 but it was ugly and Mallett let us have it in the change room afterwards. He felt we should have buried Australia and had used up all our luck because we had got the win, but, as was his way, he did manage to soften the outburst by reminding us we were the first Springbok team to win a Test in Australia since 1993, and the first to ever win a Tri Nations match against the Wallabies in Australia. We were now 11 from 11 but also, only seven days away from playing the All Blacks in Wellington, New Zealand.

Mallett demanded an overall improvement in our game execution if we had any price of being the first Springboks to win a Test in New Zealand since our return from international isolation. The best result had been the 18-all draw in Auckland in the third and final Test in 1994 and Andre Markgraaff and Carel du Plessis' teams had lost in 1996 and 1997.

He told us to enjoy the celebration in Perth but to be professional about our alcohol intake because the flight to Wellington was seven hours and there was also a five-hour time difference. Our recovery was going to be decisive if we were going to challenge the All Blacks in their own backyard.

We partied in Perth but there was calm to how we celebrated and I didn't have to worry about Peter Conway and Rob Reynolds rocking up in Perth and beating the crap out of some locals in the hotel car park.

SOARING WITH THE BOKS

There is something very special about being a Springbok in New Zealand for a showdown with the All Blacks and there is something empowering as a South African player to arrive in New Zealand when the locals make you the favourite to beat the All Blacks.

That's the position we found ourselves in as Springboks when we got to Wellington in 1998. The All Blacks, so successful in 1996 and 1997, were under siege from their own people and their own media. It wasn't something I'd seen before and I don't think it is something too many visiting players ever get to see.

We were unbeaten in 11 Tests and we knew we had a very good team. Nick Mallett had settled on a starting pack that he trusted and the tight five was one of the best, if not the best, I would know in my international career. We were an all-English front row in loosehead prop Robbie Kempson, myself and tighthead prop Adrian Garvey. We were also an understated front row because on the surface we didn't have that imposing larger-than-life look, but you won't find tougher props than Kempson and Garvey. They could do the basics of prop play as good as anyone I have played with or against and they could rumble with the best of them. What I loved about both of them was that they were two of the nicest guys off the field. Garvey was originally from Zimbabwe and he was just one of those guys that you couldn't help but love. I think even the opposition loved him as a person. There was nothing to dislike about Garvey, the person, but as a rugby player he was as tough as you can get. Kempson was schooled in the Eastern Cape and was very cultured in that he could play the piano and was into show jumping. Yes, you are allowed a chuckle when imagining a Springbok loosehead prop enjoying the pleasures of clearing hurdles on horseback in his white tights and riding cap. Seriously, though, I enjoyed my Springbok time with Kempson on my left and Garvey on my right. They could play and they could mix it with anyone, but they were just such good guys off the field. The three of us were South Africa's front-row combination in one of the most successful eras and of those who have played more than 20 Tests for South Africa, only Morne du Plessis (86 percent) and Garvey (82 percent) bettered my 81-percent win rate.

The All Blacks, so dominant in 1996 and 1997, struggled in 1998 and they slumped to five successive Tests, which hasn't happened since. One of those defeats was against us in Wellington in the last Test played at the old Athletic Park.

I had been at Athletic Park during the Bok tour of New Zealand in 1994. It's a dump. There's no other way to describe the playing facility. Back in 1994, the Springboks had beaten Wellington in a tour match and lost the second Test 13-9, which would decide the series. But in 1998, 17 years after Naas Botha had kicked the Boks to victory at the very same ground in the second Test of the 1981 series, we'd create our own history and win.

The All Blacks were high in quality players but low on confidence and their losing sequence proved that it didn't matter who you were, when the confidence of players went, so did everything else. They were also a team without Sean Fitzpatrick for the first time in 10 years and it showed. Anton Oliver, Fitzpatrick's successor, was a decent player but he was no Fitzpatrick and Taine Randell, as a captain, didn't command any presence.

New Zealanders will argue they should easily have beaten us because Carlos Spencer missed five penalties in the first 40 minutes, but having been at the coalface of this contest for 80 minutes I can tell you there was no way they were beating us. The All Blacks weren't good enough on the day and our pack was too strong for them. The results of big Test matches are determined by who wins the collisions and who controls the set piece, and at Athletic Park we were always controlling both, especially in defence. Pieter Muller, at inside centre, was colossal that day. I think he put in 21 tackles and each time he hit an All Black they all felt it. I don't think South Africans realise just how strong the Springboks were at the time and I wonder how many appreciate the quality in that Springbok squad. The Bok pack would be the equal of any that played before or has come afterwards and you'd struggle to leave Joost van der Westhuizen, Henry Honiball and Pieter Muller out of any all-time Springboks best XV. Defensively, you won't get a more imposing No 9, 10 and 12 to have ever played the game. Individually, there was talent in our team but the biggest strength was the collective of the side. We played for each other and we played as a team. You have to credit Mallett for his selections because he identified a pack right from the beginning of his tenure and, in that first year, he picked that combination in every Test. The only time he would change was when a player was injured. He applied a similar principle among the backs and the more we won, the more he rewarded each player with selection.

The All Blacks were very good that day, but we were better. We had greater confidence and more settled combinations. We weren't playing for survival, but they were. They were desperate but they were missing Fitzpatrick's experience as a leader and his skills at hooker. Oliver simply wasn't in the class of Fitzpatrick as a player. Randell was also no Zinzan Brooke as a No 8 and we simply didn't rate Randell as a player, let alone an All Blacks captain. We found him to be soft.

We knew we had to play with an intensity unrivalled in our previous 11 successive wins to triumph in New Zealand, and we did. Defensively, it was one of the most satisfying Test matches I've ever played in and tactically it was also one of the most intelligent.

We were so confident we would win and as the week progressed in the build-up, our confidence continued to grow. Mallett, like us, didn't lack for positivity in the Test week and if he had been brutal with his criticism in the immediate moment after we beat Australia, he was brilliant in how he built us up over the week for the Wellington Test. He believed in us as much as we believed in ourselves.

What I loved so much about the Test was the respect between the two teams in the build-up, during the match and afterwards. The one thing about the All Blacks is you get the same humility from their players after the game, regardless of whether they have won or lost. There is never any moaning, blaming of the referee or bitterness from the players. Their media may be different and their supporters may take defeat badly but the players are absolute warriors on the field and gentlemen once the final whistle goes.

The All Blacks coach, John Hart came into our changing room afterwards to congratulate Nick and also to tell us players how deserving we were of beating New Zealand. The All Blacks would share a beer with us and give us our dues as victors. Nick allowed the travelling South African media into our change room and everyone toasted the occasion. I'd never experienced the South African media as an ally but in Wellington, in this dungeon that doubled as a change room, I was as happy to see them as they were to see me. It really was a great day and one very few players touring New Zealand ever get to experience. Momentarily, I felt happy but I knew it was only in a rugby sense; emotionally I was a mess because of the break up with Shelley.

Earlier in the week I had met with Nick to discuss the new SA Rugby contracts. I was among a handful of survivors of the 1995 World Cup-winning squad who had enjoyed the privilege of three-year contracts. Nick could see I was distracted and he still took the piss out of me as to the category of my future contract. I only know this because when I didn't react to him putting me in a lower category bracket, he corrected it and questioned if I was paying attention.

Frankly, I didn't really care. I had never known loss like I did with Shelley and I was suffering from a broken heart. It was the most terrible of feelings and it didn't matter what I did, all I could think about was Shelley.

Wellington, in 1994, was an awful memory because of the series loss and our betrayal, as a squad, of Johan le Roux, who would be banned for biting Fitzpatrick's ear. The last time I had been in the city as a Springbok we'd left Johan behind to fight his own battle, and I was on the bus that drove away from him. I have always felt disgust and shame that we never rallied behind him in 1994, but when we left Wellington in 1998, I felt proud to be among those Springboks who had beaten the All Blacks. I felt so good to be on that bus.

Nick spoke to the squad about humility and perspective. He said the win would mean nothing more than a glorified 80 minutes if we didn't finish the job against the All Blacks and Australia in South Africa. He wanted us to be proud of the win but he urged us to only celebrate when we'd beaten Australia at Ellis Park to claim South Africa's first Tri Nations title.

There was such leadership among the Springboks that he didn't have to explain himself. The boys enjoyed the festivities in Wellington but it was all within reason and there was nothing untoward or over the top when it came to the post-match drinks.

We had a job to do in South Africa and we would have some home time before playing the All Blacks in Durban.

I tried to focus my energy on the chemical business when we got back and I tried to limit my time with Peter Conway and Rob Reynolds. I confided in my friend Camillo that I was depressed and heart-broken and I knew I could speak to him without being judged. Just talking to Camillo was a release and he encouraged me to enjoy the off-time and recharge the batteries for what could be the greatest fortnight of my rugby career.

The All Blacks had won the 1996 and 1997 Tri Nations titles and the Auckland Blues had won the Super Rugby titles in the same period. The All Blacks had also beaten everyone on tour in Europe and the United Kingdom and, in 1996, they'd won a series in South Africa for the first time. They were the premier team in world rugby but they were also a team we'd already beaten and we got a sense they were a team of players confused by selections and who, for the first time in their international careers, were doubting their ability.

Mallett was concerned that there were three weeks between our Wellington win and the Durban Test. I think he wanted to play the All Blacks in the return match the next day because South African players can get ahead of themselves and not deliver when expected to do so. I've seen it so often - the Boks can win a Test in which no one gives them a chance but the moment they're made to be the favourites, the players crumble under the weight of expectation.

Mallett went big on this and said that what defined great teams was that they delivered when the world expected it. He asked us if we felt we were a better team than New Zealand and we were unanimous that we were. He asked how many teams could keep the All Blacks tryless in New Zealand. That is how good we were, but we needed to show our own people, at home in South Africa, that the Wellington win wasn't a fluke.

What was so effective about Nick's first year in charge was his consistency in selection and the only change he made for Durban from the Wellington win was restoring a fit Rassie Erasmus at flank. The rest of the team was the one that knew how it felt to beat the All Blacks and also knew what it took to beat them.

The All Blacks made lots of changes and the most significant was picking Isitolo Maka at No 8. He was huge and very physical and it meant we were going to get a very different challenge from Wellington when the All Blacks started with Randell at No 8. Randell played flank in Durban but Maka was the big difference in their performance in the opening hour.

They dominated the first half and led 17-5 at half time. Mallett was livid but credit has to be given to the All Blacks because they played with an intent that had been missing from the Wellington match. Their pack stood up to us and Andrew Mehrtens, with front-foot ball, was starting to show his class at flyhalf.

Mallett was hectic in blasting us but Gary was calm in delivering the message. We had to put in a bigger effort up front and win some ball for our backs, who had to back themselves on attack. We also had to believe in our fitness and conditioning.

What followed was 40 of the most intense minutes of Test rugby, in which we scored four tries and turned a 17-5 deficit into a 24-23 win. I scored one of the four tries and the first question I always get asked when speaking at rugby dinners is whether I scored or not. My answer is always that it's in the books, but I reckon I may have been short and if the Television Match Official system was in place, the try would have been disallowed.

It was my fifth try in a Test match and it would be the last time I'd ever score for the Springboks. I didn't know this at the time and the thought never crossed my mind because I was convinced that I'd play 100 Tests for South Africa.

What mattered was that we had beaten the All Blacks twice in the space of one month and we were one win away from the Tri Nations title. We certainly didn't rate the Wallabies as much as we did the All Blacks, but we couldn't deny that they had given us a scare in Perth where we'd won by just one point.

Nick and Gary were worried that the players may be unable to raise their game after the high of beating the All Blacks but they needn't have been concerned because every player understood the individual responsibility of us, as a team, turning the Tri Nations campaign into a championship-winning one.

Australia had some wonderful backline players but we didn't rate their pack as highly as we did their backs. Nick trusted the same team that won in Durban to win in Johannesburg, and we had no doubt we would win.

Rugby was consuming me because I wanted it to consume me. I just wanted to get this one match out of the way, win the title and then cut loose in my home town of Johannesburg. I'd played all my senior provincial rugby out of Ellis Park and that's where I'd been in the side that had beaten the All Blacks in 1996 and then the British and Irish Lions in 1997. It was only appropriate that we would beat the Wallabies at Ellis Park in 1998 and win the Tri Nations for the first time in what I consider South Africa's most celebrated and famous stadium.

The match was billed as a final and we gave it the respect any Springbok player would give a major final. South Africa's rugby fans treated it as if it was a World Cup final, with 62 000 filling Ellis Park for a day that would start with anticipation and end with celebration.

I rated our second-half performance as the most clinical in our season and we turned a 16-12 lead into a decisive 29-15 win. Percy Montgomery kicked like a champion, good old Garvey got on the scoreboard and Bobby Skinstad scored a spectacular try.

There was nothing more for Mallett to say and there was nothing for us to do but go large.

It was the craziest of times to be playing international rugby; I was in a team that won the Tri Nations for the first time and, in the course of the year, went on to equal the then world record of 17 successive wins.

This was a Springbok squad that would beat every team over a 12-month period between 1997 and 1998, but it was also a team made up of so many contrasting characters, many of whom were young, impressionable and immersed in the nightlife culture. We trained hard but we partied as hard. We loved our rugby and we knew we were the best in the world at that stage, but we all had our vices. For some it was alcohol. For others it was ecstasy and cocaine.

DRUGS, RUCKS AND ROLLS

The recreational drug culture was big in rugby from 1997 and was at a peak among players within the Springbok squad at the end of 1998, when I would play my last Test matches under Nick Mallett.

On the Saturday night we beat Australia at Ellis Park to win the 1998 Tri Nations title, Johannesburg was always going to struggle to contain our appetite for fun and for freedom after the intensity of the two-month campaign.

I was among those who combined Test match celebrations with booze and recreational substances back then, and there were three groups of players when it came to recreational substance users: those who only did ecstasy, those who only did cocaine and a handful who did both.

Some did it more regularly than others but it was rife in the rugby culture and it wasn't confined to South African players. Because of my association with Peter Conway, Rob Reynolds and the Hells Angles, I had easy access to whatever any player wanted. Some handled the situation better than others.

There were players in the squad who were absorbed by the idea of those dark alleys when it comes to the Johannesburg nightlife and others who privately courted a more extended introduction and stay, and never said no to any invitation to indulge. There was never any testing for recreational drug use before 2000 and players who used would always believe it would be flushed out of their system with a good training session the next day.

Springbok rugby players are a drawcard at any nightclub in South Africa, but not always for the right reasons. You have those people who want to hang with the players because it gives them some form of status on the night and access to the VIP areas, and then you have those guys who see fighting a Springbok as giving them permanent status. These pricks, who seek out a fight, always do so with the knowledge that the player is unlikely to hit first because of the possible damage to his career.

I was aware of these possible pitfalls in the various clubs for those Springbok players who weren't based in Johannesburg but I liked the nightlife scene. They had to be protected and I'd take it on myself to ensure there wouldn't be issues when the players were out on the town. Peter Conway and Rob Reynolds would make sure the players were treated as untouchables at specific clubs and the players would be given the royal treatment of never having to queue and never having to worry about taking a beating. They were protected by Johannesburg's elite enforcers and if ecstasy or cocaine was their poison for the night, it was discreetly arranged. You'd get the odd player who'd lose the plot because of an inability to handle himself while hammered but there were always measures in place to ensure it didn't become an issue, at the club or in the media the following day.

I was like the Pied Piper for many players when we were in Johannesburg and the first questions I'd get from some of them would be about when, where and what. Springbok players always feel entitled when they are making the team on a regular basis and they love being feted and celebrated wherever they go, but some of them had to learn that this entitlement didn't carry over into that other darker world they craved, even if this craving was only for a Wednesday or Saturday night.

It was a world like nothing they knew because it was fraught with danger and temptation, but it was an environment that excited some of them in those brief moments that they got to observe it from a protected distance. The odd player abused the introductions and the excess that was available and there was an incident when a prominent player had racked up a R30 000 cocaine bill on behalf of Peter Conway and myself.

Conway loved the idea of having the Springboks around and when he was entertaining them, he would have taken a bullet for any of them but don't take his drugs and not pay him and don't take his drugs and *say* you'll pay. There is honour among thieves and there is also retribution to those who don't understand that even in this world of anarchy, there are rules.

Conway didn't tolerate anyone who messed with his drugs supply, whether it was a senior Hells Angel, or a Springbok rugby player. There was an occasion when I was present when Rob Reynolds had been sent to teach one of the veteran Hells Angels a lesson because this particular Angel had been using the ecstasy pills instead of selling them. I happened to be visiting this person when Rob arrived and it took a lot of talking from me to convince Rob that there was a solution outside of facial reconstruction of a mate. That situation was eventually calmed and I would also manage to soothe Peter when it came to the lesson that he wanted to teach one of the Springboks. I convinced him to write off the R30 000 debt and promised him that the player would never again do it.

I tried to educate the players who wanted in on the nightlife scene about the dos and don'ts of that world, and mostly they were well behaved.

Recreational drug use wasn't confined to South African players or being in South Africa and there were occasions overseas when players would indulge either on the Wednesday night before a Test or on the Saturday night after the Test.

England's Lawrence Dallaglio, one of the gems among the many men I played international rugby against, was a tough player and a charismatic individual, and he was very connected to the London nightlife scene. Whenever we were in London we'd chat and he'd arrange for the players to be given the VIP treatment at the best clubs. On one particular night, in the build-up to the England Test at the end of 1998, some players had asked me to arrange entrance to a club on London's West End. It was a night that I wasn't going to be with them.

I contacted Lawrence and he said he would sort the boys out but later that evening he called me horrified that one of the players had walked in and confronted a bouncer wanting to know where the drugs were.

"What the fuck kind of question is that?" Lawrence asked me.

I agreed with him and it showed the immaturity with some players when it came to their sense of entitlement and inability to even consider the consequences. Needless to say, the next time he would arrange anything, by way of VIP treatment, it was on the condition that I was there to make sure there wouldn't be another such embarrassment.

You are probably asking what about the Springbok management at the time and questioning if they knew? The answer is they did nothing because it was never brought up in a team environment and I'd like to think it was because they were oblivious to anything outside of preparing a team to play Test rugby. I don't think it was a case of ignoring the situation because we were on a winning streak and I also don't think it was out of a fear that they'd be opening a Pandora's Box and would be unable to cope with the consequences. I always got the sense they just didn't know it was going on.

Nick Mallett's only priority was to win Test matches and his focus on the 1998 end-of-year tour was breaking New Zealand's world record of 17 successive Test wins. The Springboks were unbeaten in 14 matches and it seemed as though the Hollywood script was being written for us to break the world record with a Grand Slam tour success.

Ordinarily, we should have strolled through our last competitive month of 1998 but we were a bunch of players who had given everything in a 12-month period - the body was aching and the mind was tired.

Mallett had also, for the first time in 12 months, cast doubt in the minds of the senior players who had won him 14 successive Test matches. At our first training session in Johannesburg before leaving for the United Kingdom he told the squad that no player's position was safe and that no player should take Test match selection for granted. Mallett had picked a talented and youthful midweek squad, who he said would be playing for Saturday Test places as well.

Mallett had never used this kind of approach on us since taking over in late 1997. He had never threatened players that their positions may be in doubt and his biggest selection strength in the first year was that he also gave his first-choice players security, and they in turn would reward him with performance and a winning result.

The last time we had been together as a squad, Mallett and the players were euphoric at winning the Tri Nations and giving Australia a lesson on how to close out a Test match. Now, just a few months later, he was telling the very same players there would be no Test match guarantees.

In that moment, the bond between player and coach weakened and it would never again be as strong.

The tour started with a Test against Wales at the old Wembley soccer stadium, then Scotland at Murrayfield, Ireland at Lansdowne Road and ended with what we anticipated would be the world-record win against England at Twickenham.

In 1999, South Africa's schedule involved Tests against Canada and Italy and the team management was confident that, once we added these four Tests to our winning sequence, we'd become the first Tier One team to win 20-plus Tests in a row.

Unfortunately, Mallett's motivation from the outset became the world record and that is where he got it wrong. He became obsessed with breaking New Zealand's record, when we should have stuck with the formula of wanting to win the next Test. The pressure of the record started becoming a negative and it added to what had already been a mentally draining year. Everyone, within the team, the media and fans, was thinking about it and the international broadcaster CNN was with us to do a documentary on us breaking the world record. It was as if we had already done it.

The humility within the squad, which had been a trademark of our 1997 European tour and the 1998 Tri Nations, had been replaced with an arrogance. There was also the Bobby Skinstad situation, with the media calling for Skinstad to be picked on the basis of an excellent Currie Cup season.

Skinstad was supremely talented and skilled and he had done well for South Africa when coming off the bench, but he was never going to have the same impact starting for the Springboks. He could destroy tired legs and minds in the last 30 minutes of the game with his range of skills but he weakened the sum total of our starting pack because he couldn't do the grunt work of a player like Andre Venter. Skinstad also didn't command respect from within the team like Venter did, and the senior players felt he still needed to do his international apprenticeship.

The Skinstad selection hung over the squad like a heavy cloud all tour and Mallett eventually succumbed to media pressure and the influence of his assistant coach Alan Solomons and included Skinstad in the Test starting XV. The player to miss out was Andre Venter, who was the most popular and respected forward in our pack.

Venter would still be part of the Test match-day squad but he was also picked to play in the midweek team. Typical of the player, he took it on the chin and would give his all for both teams, but it caused an immediate rift between the senior players and Skinstad. If you had asked every one of the starting forwards who they wanted playing, the answer would have been Andre Venter to run on, and Bobby Skinstad to come off the bench.

We had the formula up front, at the end of 1997 and into 1998, and Nick tampered with it. He tried to fix something that was never broken, and there was no reason to mess with what was working.

Mallett underestimated team dynamics in his haste to include Skinstad and he didn't factor in how destructive it would be to the forward unit that had proven itself the best in the world over a one-year period.

We were a disjointed squad on the 1998 end of season tour and you just couldn't compare the environment or the spirit to the fantastic European tour at the same time a year earlier. The tour of 1997 was such a joy and we played with such freedom. Now every day was proving to be a chore. The players were physically and mentally jaded and many in the squad were feeling undermined.

While the midweek team was smashing inferior opposition, the Test team was stumbling through the opening fortnight of the tour.

Wales, with a new coach in Graham Henry, had picked their strongest team at Wembley and it may as well have been a different country from the imposters who nearly took 100 points against us in Pretoria. We sneaked in 28-20 and we'd also stutter in beating Scotland 35-10.

The hype around the Irish Test was big because of the brutal battle of Pretoria and the Irish had told us when they left South Africa that they'd be waiting for us in Dublin. We'd told them, through Gary Teichmann, that we looked forward to being in Dublin to give them another beating in their own backyard.

My showdown with Keith Wood was among the talking points all week in Dublin and I knew I would be a target for the Irish. The challenge of Wood naturally refreshed my mind, if only for a few days, and I wanted to make it three from three after dominating him in Bloemfontein and Pretoria.

My pre-Test ritual has always been to train every day, even when the squad has an off-day. It's always been this way for me, even when I was at school. I wanted to be the fittest and the best conditioned and my father had always instilled in me that I'd get an edge if I was training when my opponent was resting.

My training on the rest day would include a session on the treadmill and in this particular week I felt my hamstring tighten and tear while I was on the treadmill. I knew I was out of the Test and went to see the medical team, and then I told Mallett. He was furious with me and asked why I was training when the team was off. I told him he'd never questioned it in the build-up to every Test over the past year and he said he didn't care what it took but I would be starting. He said it was important Ireland saw me running out and that Wood knew I would be playing.

The medical team worked my hamstring in the 24 hours before the Test, strapped it tight and sent me out to conquer Wood and Ireland. Mentally I was fragile because I knew my hamstring was gone. My body also felt broken and sore. I knew I wasn't the only one in our pack taking physical strain. Mentally so many players had also spoken of exhaustion. It was proving a struggle to peak again after the high of the Tri Nations.

I lasted 12 minutes and nearly suffered the embarrassment of Wood running over me. I managed to hang on in the tackle but it was a feeble attempt to stop him and I had to accept that if I continued to play that I'd be a passenger. I'd be doing myself and the team a disservice and I left the field.

My departure angered Mallett who felt I had let him and the team down. It was the start of the end in our relationship which had been strong for a year.

The Boks beat Ireland in a match that lacked the brutality of Pretoria and we were again too skilled and too good a rugby team to lose to them. We had equalled the All Blacks world record of 17 successive Test wins and would finally socialise over a few beers with the Irish squad at the plush Burlington Hotel, which was our base.

Players from both teams were big enough to put aside whatever issues there may have been from the Pretoria Test and the Irish players wanted us to beat England the next week as much as we felt we would.

On the Monday following the Ireland victory, in the week of the England Test, I got a call from one of my mates in Johannesburg. He told me that Mallett had climbed into me in the Afrikaans media and that newspaper posters had Mallett calling me dumb and stupid.

The comments hurt me and I sought Mallett out to tell him how I felt. He was still seething that I had damaged my hamstring on the treadmill but I was angry that he had disrespected me in the media. The headline in the newspaper was as humiliating as it was insulting and our relationship as coach and player would never be the same.

I wasn't in a position to play against England because my hamstring was gone. Mallett refused to accept it and said the medical team could get me right and that I had to play through the pain.

I knew it had nothing to do with mind over matter because my body was broken. If I was a car then my chassis was bent. I should never have agreed to play.

Mallett had also called me in to tell me he thought I was a negative influence on Percy Montgomery and that Montgomery

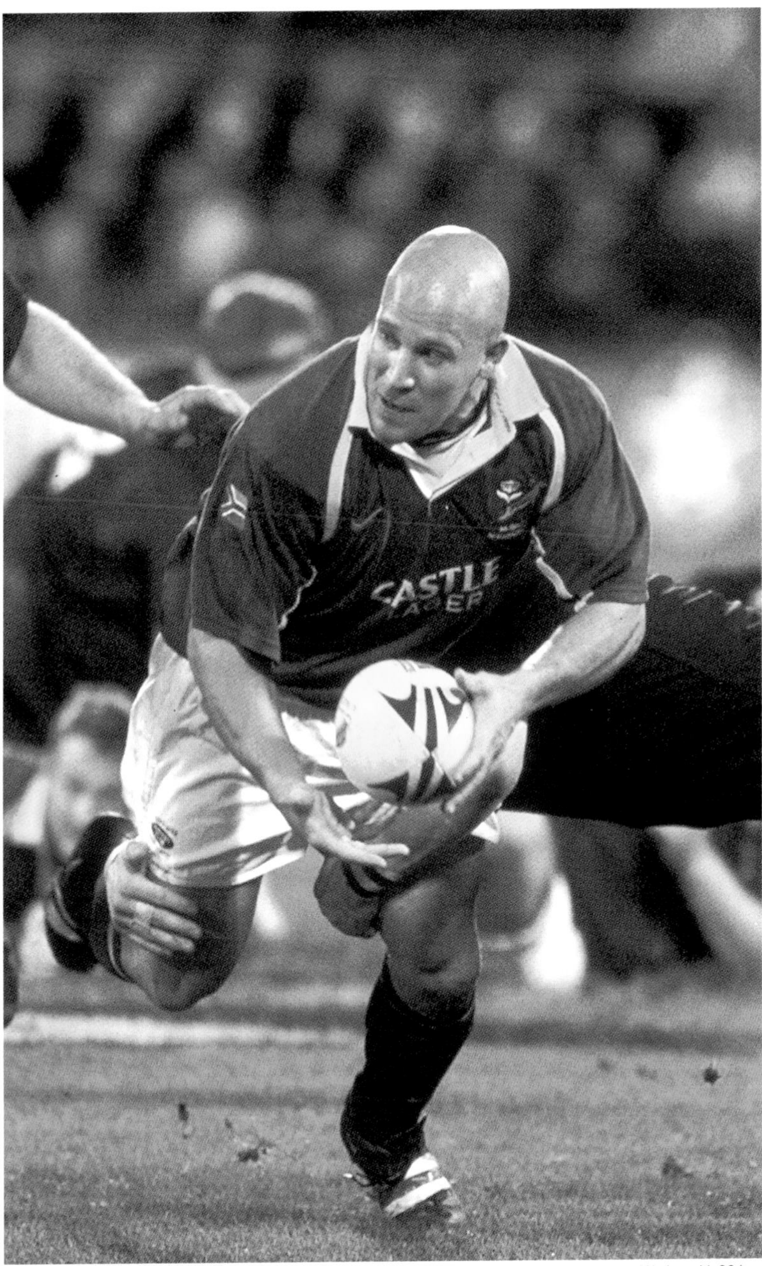

Looking to get an offload away to a support runner in what was my last Test in New Zealand. We lost 41-20 in Wellington (2002).
(Photo by Nigel Marple/Getty Images)

TOP: Pumping those legs and licking my lips as I lined up that poor French winger in Bordeaux during a 22-12 win for the Boks in November, 1996.
Mike Cooper/Allsport

BELOW: I got the better of Will Greenwood here, but the England centre had the last laugh after they smashed us 53-3 at Twickenham (23 November, 2002).
(Photo by Stephen Munday/Getty Images)

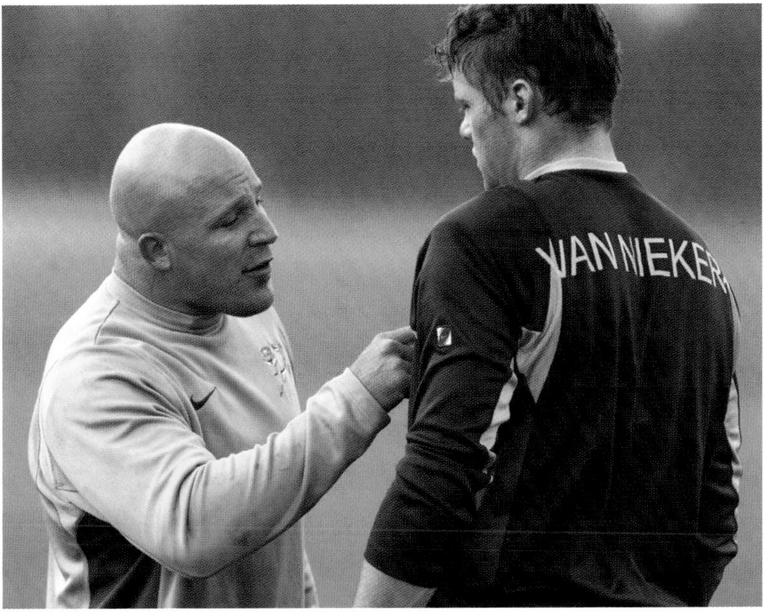

TOP: Sharing a few words of wisdom with Joe van Niekerk during the build-up to what would be my last appearance for South Africa, against England at Twickenham in November, 2002.
(Photo by Touchline Photo/Getty Images) Touchline Photo images are available to clients in the UK, USA and Australia only.

BELOW: I played 10 Currie Cup matches for the Lions in 1999, here we beat Western Province 37-22 at the Danie Craven Stadium in Stellenbosch.
Galloimages

Making small talk with the ref while England hooker Richard Cockerill tries to catch his breath before a scrum at Twickenham (November, 1997).
David Rogers/Allsport

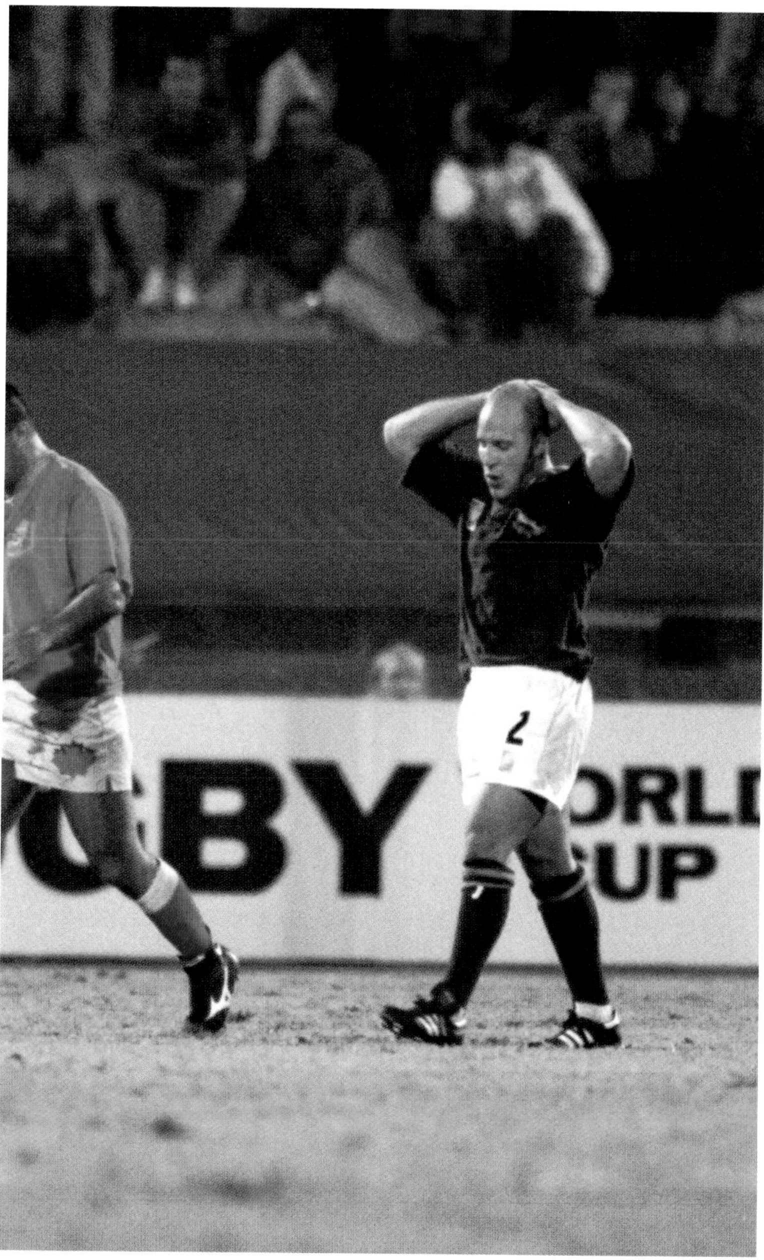

Even though I didn't throw a punch, I was sent off for trying to stop the fight at the Boet Erasmus Stadium. My 1995 World Cup was over.
(Photo by Tony Marshall/EMPICS via Getty Images)

Slipping out of a tackle during a Super 12 match for the Bulls against the Chiefs.
Galloimages

Powering into a tackle by All Blacks flanker Richie McCaw as we opened the 2002 Tri Nations tournament with a 41-20 loss in Wellington.
(Photo by Ross Land/Getty Images)

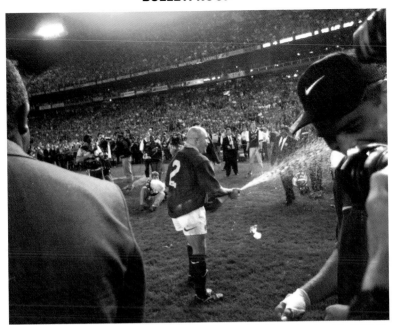

TOP: The champagne flowed on and off the field after we beat Australia in Johannesburg to put South Africa's name on the Tri Nations trophy for the first time.

BELOW: We started the 1998 Test season by steamrolling Ireland 37-13 in Bloemfontein.
Galloimages

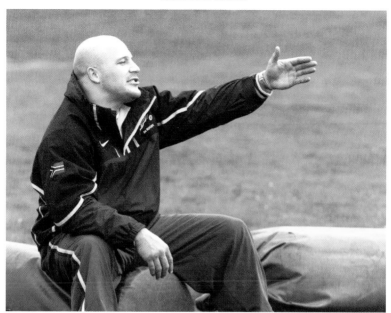

TOP: Coaching has always come naturally to me!
Galloimages

BELOW: Try-time against the Canterbury Crusaders, the Super 12's worst team in 1996.
Galloimages

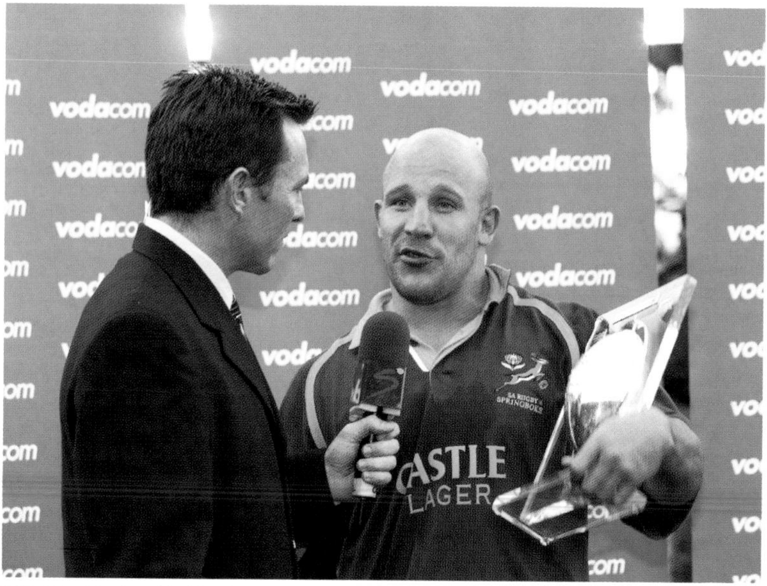

TOP: Being interviewed by 1995 Rugby World Cup teammate Joel Stransky after a man-of-the-match performance for South Africa.
Galloimages

BELOW: Showing off my passing skills with a pass across the face of Wallabies captain John Eales during the Tri Nations match in Perth in 1998.
David Rogers/Allsport

Belting out the national anthem at the 1995 Rugby World Cup.
Galloimages

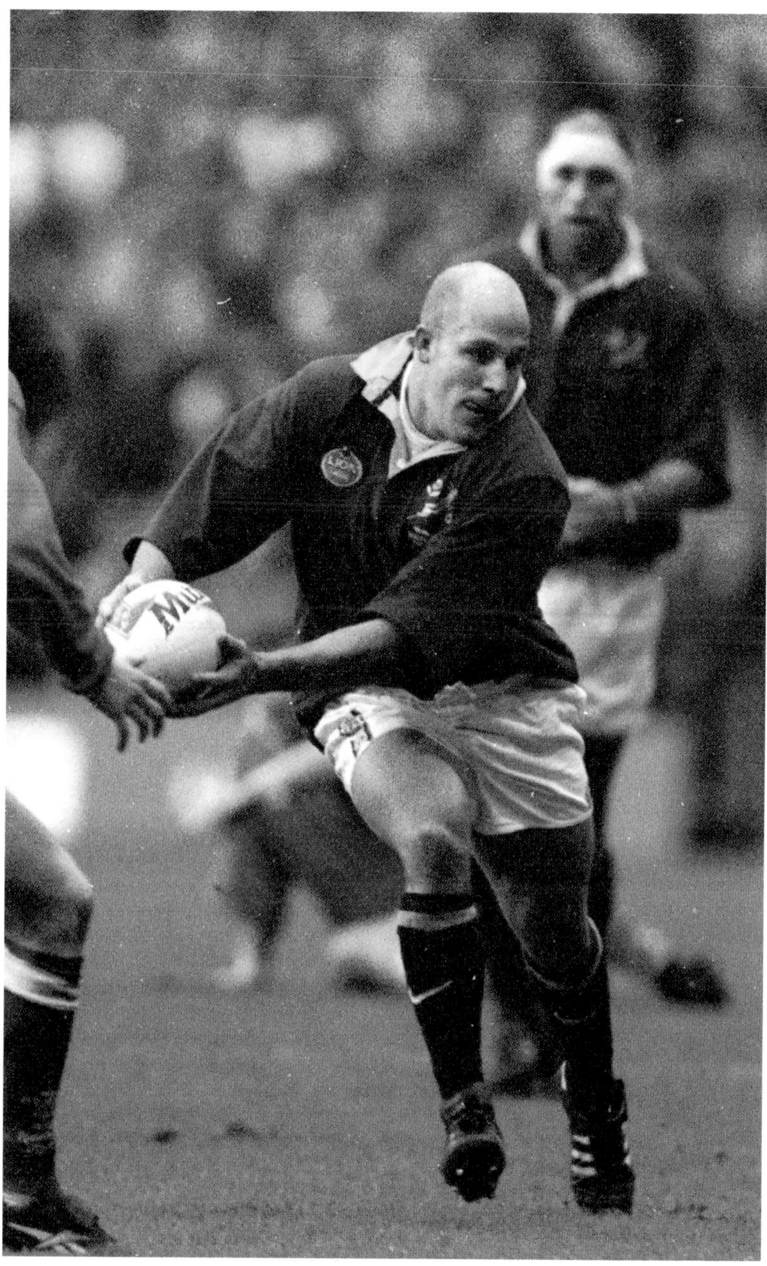

Making a break down the short side against Wales at Cardiff Arms Park with a young Neil Jenkins very relieved that I was looking to pass.
Galloimages

TOP: Great banter with Bok loose forward Warren Brosnihan at a function.
Galloimages

BELOW: Catching up with John Smit and Victor Matfield at the Wanderers Club after the funeral service for James Small.
(Photo by Lee Warren/Gallo Images)

TOP: Here I am in my Bok blazer, posing for a photo with Mac (who gave me my first call-up to the national team) and scrumhalf Johan Roux.
Galloimages

BELOW: Cooling off in the pool with Brent Russell (L) and Breyton Paulse (R) in one of Rudolf Straeuli's 'bonding' exercises.
Galloimages

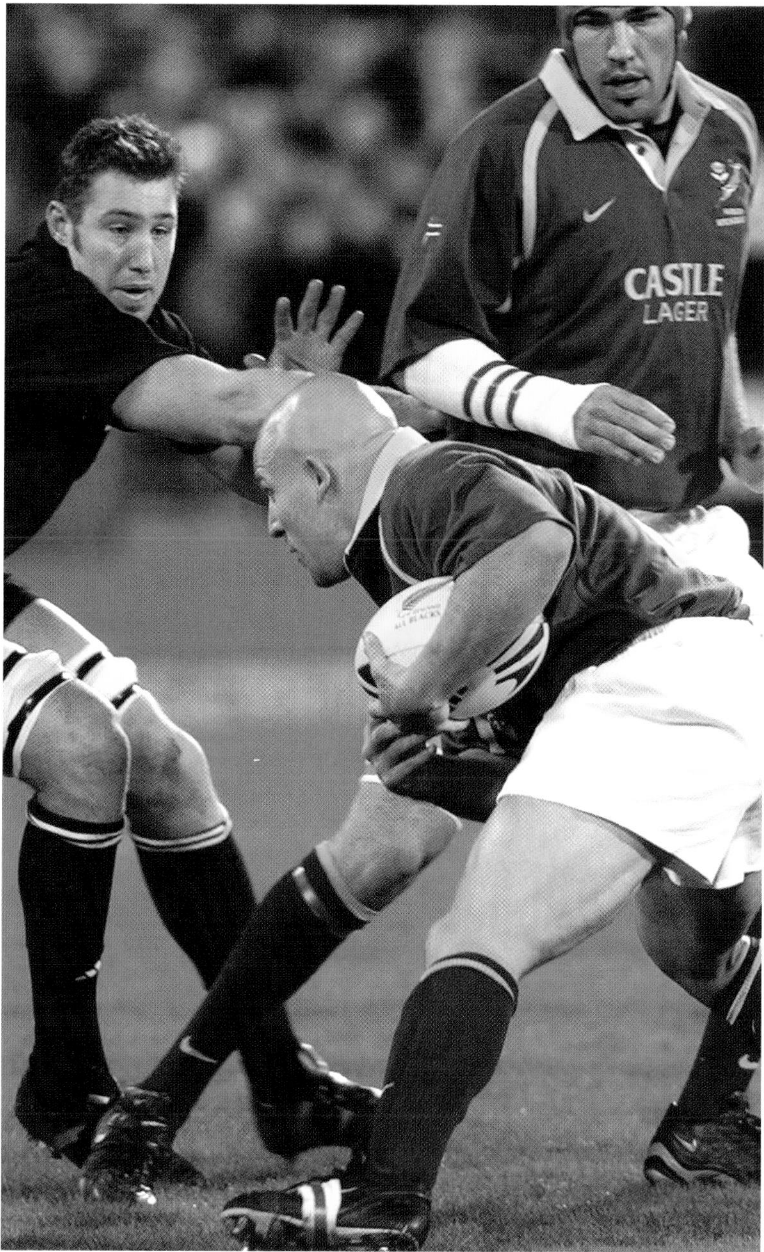

Ducking into the gap outside All Blacks lock Chris Jack with Victor Matfield watching on during the 2002 Tri Nations loss against New Zealand in Wellington.
(Photo by Ross Land/Getty Images)

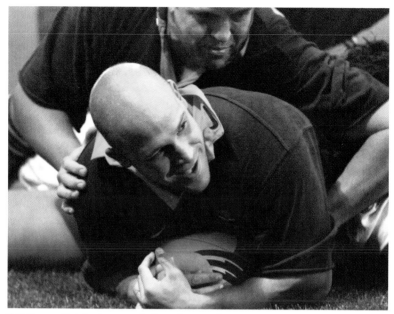

TOP: Krynauw Otto helped me across the line and I was very happy after scoring this try to beat France in Lyon during the second match of our 1997 tour to Europe.
Galloiimages

BELOW: I'm at the bottom of that pile scoring a try against New Zealand in the 1998 Tri Nations match at Kings Park. We won 24-23.
Galloiimages

wasn't emotionally equipped to deal with my dominant personality. He feared Montgomery would lose his way and his focus by trying to imitate me. Mallett even went as far as banning me from sitting near Monty during meals.

My last week on tour was turning into a mess and Lawrence Dallaglio's phone call to me was another complication I could have done without. Just three days before we were to play England at Twickenham and hopefully break the world record for successive wins, I was trying to get myself into a space where I could take the field and now I was having to manage the potential fall out of a Springbok player stupidly walking into a nightclub and asking a bouncer to arrange drugs for him.

We had won 17 Tests in a row and I'd started in every one of them. What should have been the crowning glory was starting to just feel gory. England had selected all their best players and we knew that only our best would be good enough but I knew that there was no way I could give my best.

We lost 13-7 and while there was only six points on the scoreboard, we were never in control of the Test. England deserved the win and I felt deserving of a break.

I was over Mallet and over rugby. What I had never considered was that Mallett was over me.

TAKING MY EYE OFF THE BALL

When the final whistle blew in 1998, I believed I was the best hooker in the world. Playing through a hamstring injury to face Ireland at Lansdowne Road and then England at Twickenham was a mistake but at the end of that season I had no reason to doubt what I'd achieved between the Springbok tour of Europe in 1997 and winning the Tri-Nations in 1998.

Between August of 1997 and the end of November 1998, I played 17 consecutive Tests for the Springboks without a single defeat. But in 1999 and 2000, I didn't play any Test rugby and my professional playing time was limited to 15 matches for the Lions in the Currie Cup and Vodacom Cup competitions. The best hooker in the world was playing Vodacom Cup rugby, when I should have been at the 1999 World Cup and dominating world rugby in 2000.

How?

It's all my fault.

I lost control after the 1998 end-of-season tour. I was drained, disillusioned and fed up but mostly I was still heartbroken. Shelley had crushed me like no individual or Test team could in my history of playing international rugby. I just couldn't get her out of my system and, out of nothing other than impulse and immaturity, I asked Camillo and Percy Montgomery to accompany me on a boat cruise from Cape Town to Brazil during the summer of 1998/99.

What followed was three weeks of indulgence and decadence and when I returned to South Africa for the preseason, I was a mess. Typically, I didn't recognise the situation. I hadn't trained for the three weeks that I had been on a bender between Cape Town and Brazil and I justified the trip as a necessary release after 12 of the most intense months of rugby and relationship issues.

Now I found myself back in training for the 1999 Super Rugby season and I just wasn't ready. It was the first time I found myself in a situation where I hadn't put in the work to be ready to play. For all of my poor decisions and mistakes, the one certainty was that I would always be on top of my game when it came to rugby.

Now I wasn't on top of my game and it was as foreign to me as it was to everyone in rugby who knew me.

I wasn't prepared physically for a preseason camp and, in one of the first sessions, I tore whatever muscles I could in my groin because I simply wasn't in shape when I arrived for training. I'd let myself down and the player who in the past two years had been the world's best hooker was not the player who arrived at training in late January in 1999.

Any prospect of me playing in Super Rugby was put on hold and the Vodacom Cup, South Africa's second-tier domestic competition, was my lot for the first few months of 1999.

I got a sense that I was in trouble when it came to making the Springboks because of my fall out with Nick Mallett on the 1998 end-of-year tour. Though Nick and I had been tight as the Boks won his first 16 Tests in charge, it was now as if I'd never played for him. Forget that I had been his starting hooker for 12 months, there was no communication between Nick and myself in 1999 and there was very little chance of me making the World Cup squad.

It was to be my second World Cup to end prematurely, only this time it would be through non-selection and not a suspension.

I resented Nick at the time but I also had to accept responsibility for how I was playing, who I was and just where my life was positioned in 1999.

I was a fucking mess.

I would play 10 Currie Cup matches for Transvaal in 1999. Compare that to Walter Minnaar who made 31 appearances for Transvaal in 1999. I wasn't physically on top of my game and mentally I was nowhere.

My relationship breakdown with Shelley was more severe than I could ever have imagined and my chemical business was falling to pieces.

Japie Mulder, the powerful and imposing Springbok centre, who was so famous for his tackle on Jonah Lomu in the 1995 Rugby World Cup final, was my business partner. Japie was a brilliant rugby player and one of the hardest tacklers on the rugby field. His nickname was "Varkie" ("Piggy" in English) which was a nickname earned because of his uncompromising attitude and tackling on a rugby field. He could break a player in half when he made contact and he was globally recognised as one of the best centres in the 1990s. But when it came to business and taking responsibility, Japie was a pussy. He was a big disappointment in my life and remains a disappointment because he has never owned up to his business failings and never accepted culpability for his poor business decisions. He cost me a lot of money and while the anger has subsided over the years, my disgust for him as a man remains as intense.

Japie had this affectionate, dumbass smile as a rugby player, but when he flashed that smile at a board meeting, I knew we had problems when it came to our business financials.

Our chemical business hit the skids and I only found out because my mom alerted me to irregularities in a personal account that ran parallel with our business accounts. Our business traded two accounts, which included a bonus account with access to liquid cash, which Japie or I could use in the case of an emergency.

Conway Reynolds handled our finance and I had introduced him to the business around the time Japie was brought in as a partner. Reynolds was a guy who I had met through Mercedes and he was a financial director at M2 Cargo Motors in Johannesburg's northern suburbs. Reynolds had arranged for sponsored vehicles for Transvaal rugby players and that is how our relationship started.

Japie came to me after training and said he was keen on getting involved in a business and asked if I would consider a partner. I didn't have players I would call friends in rugby at the time but I liked Japie and it was an opportunity for him to acquire shares in a business. It would also be a relatively low-key entry into business and the portfolio would allow him to grow and learn as a director.

Unfortunately, over time I'd learn that Japie's business acumen was in contrast to his standing as a rugby player, and to complicate matters, the two of us trusted Reynolds way too much.

Japie and I were Springbok rugby players and the best in our position in South Africa and, when on top of our game, among the best in the world, but we were not business people and we suffered because of this naivety, Japie more than me. There is a book written about 10 000 hours of business but we had 50 000 hours of rugby between us and zero hours of business.

I started hearing rumours of Conway being dismissed from Mercedes because of irregularities and the talk was he had long fingers on those little hands of his but, when I studied the books, everything seemed in order. I spoke to Japie about the rumours and he said I was being paranoid and that Reynolds only acted in the best interests of the company. Japie was spending more time with Reynolds than I was so I took his word at face value, until I came back from the Bok tour at the end of 1998 and my mother called to say there was nothing in the additional business emergency account. I told her it couldn't be because, when I had left for the tour, there was at least R500 000 available.

She confirmed there was a zero balance and I called Reynolds and Japie to an emergency meeting, in which the reality of the zero balance was confirmed. There had been no transparency in any transactions while I was away and I was angry. What emerged was that Reynolds had set up his wife with a beauty salon and a sunbed and bought his daughter a horse. He had presented the cheques to Japie, who had signed them off in my absence. Japie, through his negligence and naivety, had never studied what the payments were for and he had signed whatever cheques Reynolds had put in front of him.

I had no recourse.

I tried to prosecute Reynolds but it was a dead end because Japie, as a director, had signed off on the cheques. At the time, while I was away on tour, Japie would handle distribution and Reynolds was in charge of finance and how it worked was that Reynolds would take the cheques to Japie for payment and Japie had signed without checking the requisition. There was no consequence to Reynolds.

Legally, there was nothing I could do, so I tried to leverage my weight with the Hells Angles and with Peter Conway to see if they could pressure Reynolds into making good on the money that he had taken from the business. All that led to was Reynolds going to the police and complaining about intimidation. Conway denied that he had said anything to Reynolds and it was the first time that I saw the coward in Conway, though that didn't mean I had seen him for all his bullshit.

Reynolds walked away unscathed and unscarred and Japie also ran a mile when it came to saving the business or watching it sink. Japie may have loved tackling but he didn't embrace conflict when it came to business. There was no accountability on his side. He signed the cheques but he insisted I was the villain.

It was the end of our friendship and our business relationship and all sorts of stories emerged, one of them being that I had beaten up Japie. Just like the story of the James Dalton jersey on Jeppe High's bell tower, this never happened. There is no jersey on the bell tower and I have never raised a hand to Japie. I loved Japie as a rugby player, was fond of him as a business partner and was starting to think of him as a friend, but the only love that remains is of him as a rugby player. He was never a friend and he took no accountability as a business partner. He didn't in 1999 and, 20 years later, he still has never admitted that he fucked up by signing cheques without checking.

My business, once a gold mine, was gone and instead of Japie and I standing together, we went our separate ways. I got such bad business advice at the time and, stupidly, I took R700 000 of my own money to pay creditors, but I was never in a position to sustain it and the business eventually went into liquidation and my money went with it.

Japie put in nothing and pleaded ignorance with that goofy smile of his. Fuck, it irked me and it still does because he has never been man enough to just stand up and say "it was me". Instead, I was left last man standing to switch the lights off.

My business was gone and my rugby was going the same way in 1999, a year in which I should have been preparing for the World Cup.

Ordinarily, my safe space would be my rugby, but even that was no longer a guarantee.

Laurie Mains, the coach of the 1995 All Blacks, was the new guy in charge at the Lions, and we clashed from the outset. Our personalities just didn't gel and Mains would coach the Lions in 1999 and take charge of the Cats in 2000 and 2001.

Mains, let me say, was a very good rugby coach. Technically and tactically, you couldn't fault him but he had no people skills, was a narcissist and when I looked at him, I saw a first-class prick and I just didn't like him. He didn't like me either and I knew that life, as I once knew it at the Lions, was no more.

Mains didn't know how to manage players and he was a bully. He also didn't like his employer, Doc Luyt, and despite the two of them agreeing on a coaching contract, Mains would spend his tenure at the Lions trying to usurp and undermine Doc Luyt.

Mains always thought I was one of Doc Luyt's boys and one of his informers. It was nonsense, but it meant that Mains and I couldn't ever find common ground.

Mains' power was that he selected the team and the players knew that their futures were dependent on selection. I frankly didn't care whether he selected me or not, which is why in 2000 I was never a consideration for his Super Rugby team, and in 1999 he reluctantly selected me when I had declared myself fit enough to play a game of rugby.

Sadly, I betrayed myself in 1999 because the James Dalton who reported for rugby duty was not the same player who had stopped Keith Wood with a smashing hit at Loftus Versfeld in 1998, or mixed it with All Blacks captain Sean Fitzpatrick at Ellis Park in 1996. The James Dalton of 1999 was a rugby imposter, but he wasn't an imposter in the dark world of Peter Conway and Rob Reynolds.

Sadly, that James Dalton was very much a regular.

'FRIENDS' NEARLY RUINED ME

Rugby was always my passion and in 1996 my passion became my profession, but three years later so many *other* things were occupying my mind and taking priority.

Missing the early part of the season through injury didn't help my mental state and only led to me spending more time with Peter Conway, Rob Reynolds and the Hells Angels. I was determined to become a fully patched member of the biker gang and I was Peter's prospect.

When I wasn't at home, I was at the Hells Angels or I was with Camillo, Julio and Carlo.

I was single so I had no responsibility, other than to myself, and my headspace was such that I had no responsibility to myself. I acted without regard for consequence and I disrespected myself as much as I did anyone else.

It's easily my darkest period and I am thankful that today I can talk about it and that I survived a year that easily could have killed me.

My chemical business was gone and my rugby seemed to be going the same way, but Conway and Reynolds weren't gone. They were stronger than they'd ever been in my life and our friendship was at a peak.

Reynolds had sold his nightclub, Global Explosion, and was investing more time in the Hells Angels and he and Conway were instrumental in relocating the Angels' Johannesburg headquarters to the Eastern Suburbs and later using it as the base for the elite charter of the Angels known as the Nomads. To be a Nomad you had to have done some serious shit and something extreme. Those in the Nomads, like Conway and Reynolds, were known as the "Filthy Few". No one messed with them and they ran the Johannesburg nightclub scene.

They bought a small hotel and turned it into a whorehouse and, as Reynolds would boast, it was an establishment that would always be filled with women. The downstairs bar was converted into a strip club and the restaurant area was the meeting room. It became a second home to me in 1999, as I hung around as a prospect and started immersing myself into being an Angel.

Julio and Carlo, who were protectors, enforcers and elite bouncers, had expanded their business interests to the illegal uncut diamond industry and they were also doing a lot of work for the Angels. The longer I spent away from rugby, the more I was finding that I didn't miss it. I was injured but was getting paid because of my contracts with the Lions and the South African Rugby Union. I knew that Nick Mallett wasn't going to pick me for the 1999 World Cup squad so I wasn't in a rush to get back onto the field.

When I did return from injury, I ended up playing 15 provincial matches and actually played well. I was amazed at my form, given that mentally I found myself lacking in desire but seemingly committed to social self-destruction.

I felt sorry for myself because of the break-up with Shelley and was lacking in emotional maturity to fix the situation. My excuse to myself was that my behaviour was acceptable because I wanted to be an Angel and I was best friends with the two most powerful Angels in Conway and Reynolds.

Conway was crazy in a lot of the things he did. So much of his behaviour was drug-induced because his nights started with booze and cocaine and those nights blurred into mornings and then back into nights.

Conway and Reynolds were the main manufacturers and distributors of narcotics to the nightclubs in Johannesburg in the late 1990s. They did it through the Angels and Peter would always justify his drug dealing by insisting that he was doing users a favour. His favourite line, if you excuse the play on the word, was: "Rather the Angels' stuff than the shit that kills people in the club from an overdose of bad stock." He would convince himself that he was righting a wrong and was some kind of narcotics saviour.

The Angels, at the time, manufactured ecstasy and distributed it mainly through the club scene and the quality of the drug was what Conway prided himself on. There was one pharmacist who fucked up a batch of pills and needless to say, he was never seen again by anyone.

There was madness when I was out with Conway, but with Julio, Carlo and Camillo it was a different kind of revelry because, with my old friends, the times were hectic but not out of control. Carlo didn't fit the bill of an enforcer at all. He was almost ginger with freckles and he looked like Archie from the comics. He was tall, had big hands, a gap in between his two front teeth and he had a potbelly. But hell, he was fearless. He wasn't an intimidating presence because he wasn't a bully and at first glance you wouldn't know what he was capable of. He was loyal to his clients and he had an ability to be emotionally detached from what he was paid to do professionally.

Julio was a mountain of a man with these sad droopy dog eyes. He didn't train much but was a karate champion and he was just as fearless as Carlo. You didn't want to mess with them and when they went calling on a job it wasn't always the prettiest of exchanges.

Camillo was doing a lot of work with Lior Saadt, the Israeli gangster, who was linked to the diamond dealer Hazel Crane and her estranged husband Shai Avissar. Avissar ran an illegal counterfeit and smuggling business in South Africa, and the smuggling mostly involved uncut diamonds.

Saadt was charged with killing Avissar, and Julio and Carlo were connected to the murder in that they helped Saadt bury Avissar somewhere near Pretoria. Carlo and Julio spoke about it to myself and Camillo, and what had happened to Avissar was an open secret in the underworld.

Conway's Hells Angels were also attracting a lot of attention from the police, and because Conway was feeling the heat he asked Julio to find a safe storage for guns and ammunition he had been keeping at the Angels headquarters. Camillo, thinking nothing of it, stored the stuff in his cupboard at the house he was sharing with me.

In the most bizarre of circumstances, Julio was arrested for driving what police claimed was a stolen car. At the time, I was doing some debt collecting with Camillo and, as part of a debt collection job, he had taken the car as security from a woman who owed his client a lot of money. The deal was that, once the money had been paid, the car would be returned. The woman reported the car as stolen and the police pulled over Camillo and arrested him for being in possession of a stolen vehicle. They then took Camillo to the house and after searching his room they found the AK-47 live ammunition, a sub machine gun, a few rifles and a few handguns.

Camillo pleaded his innocence about the car and what was in his cupboard. I was also called in by the cops as they wanted to link me to the car and the find in Camillo's cupboard. They also wanted me to look at photos of suspects in some murder cases linked to underworld activity, and asked if I was familiar with any of the suspects. I wasn't and neither was Camillo, who confirmed I had nothing to do with the storing of the guns and ammunition. Camillo called Julio to tell him what had happened and Julio said he was on his way to the cop shop. Camillo was facing a lengthy term in prison and the police had threatened to charge him with smuggling illegal weapons and with possession of illegal weapons and ammunition. Julio, to get Camillo released, made a deal with the murder and robbery detectives to take them to where Avissar was buried, at a dump somewhere near Pretoria.

Julio and Carlo would also turn state witnesses against Saadt in respect of Avissar's murder. They always joked that it had been easy to find the grave because of how lazy they had been when they buried him, as his elbow was still sticking out when they left the grave scene. They hadn't bothered to dig deeper because they were tired, and Camillo mocked them for being "such lazy, fat fucks".

Saadt went on the run and was eventually arrested and brought back to South Africa to face trial for Avissar's murder. He was also charged with two more murders and loads of other stuff. Julio and Carlo were the main state witnesses and both were assassinated in 2000 and 2001 before they could testify in court about what they had seen and what role they had played in burying Avissar, whose wife Hazel Crane was also killed in an assassination while on her way to court to testify. The investigating officer also died of a supposed heart attack and the State was forced to drop the charges against Saadt as all the main witnesses were dead.

Camillo and I don't know where Saadt is today, or even whether he's still alive.

Julio and Peter Conway's relationship had started to take strain in 2000, and Julio wasn't one to shut up to anyone, even Conway. It all came to a head over the phone while Julio and I were at Hartbeespoort Dam. The two started arguing, threats were made and Julio told me we were going to Conway's house in Sandton to sort him out.

I got hold of my dad and asked him to meet us there because I knew that this wasn't going to end well and I needed my dad's intervention in his capacity as a policeman.

Julio raced his red BMW 535 Sport to Sandton, where Conway was waiting outside for us. He was armed with an R5 rifle, was very bullish and felt protected because plenty of Hells Angels were behind him. Julio didn't give a shit because he was also armed.

My dad arrived soon after the initial showdown and ordered Conway to put the rifle down and walk with him to the garage. I don't know what they spoke about as only the two of them went into the garage. They weren't in there for long but when they came out, Conway's attitude was different. He was calm and acted as if nothing had happened. My father had saved a potentially explosive situation but nothing was going to save Conway's relationship with Julio and it would progressively get worse over the next year.

Julio's situation with Conway didn't change anything between Conway and myself. We were strong in our friendship, and it was through Conway that I met my future wife Andrea one night at the Hells Angels home base. Andrea and Conway went back a few years and when I was first introduced to her in 2000, I was hardly playing rugby, was single and she was going out with someone.

There was instant chemistry between us and I found her very sexy. She was also older than me, which I found appealing. I had not been involved with anyone since the break-up with Shelley but I respected that Andrea was in a relationship and initially didn't pursue her romantically.

She had asked me about my rugby career and questioned why I wasn't playing for the Springboks. I told her I was finished with rugby.

I had started my senior rugby career at the Lions in 1992 and would play 76 matches for them until Mains forced me to leave in 2000. I never thought I would play provincial rugby for any team and it never was a consideration that I would ever play for the Bulls or call Loftus Versfeld my home ground.

I was a born and bred Lions man.

Mains wasn't. He was an outsider, who acted like one and the only interest he had in South African rugby was furthering his own agendas.

Mains, who was coach of the Lions in 1999, was also now coaching the Cats in Super Rugby and I didn't play a game for the Cats in 2000. My rugby in 2000 consisted of five provincial matches for the Lions, which would be the last five I'd ever play for them, and one memorable afternoon in the United Kingdom playing for the British Barbarians against English champions Leicester.

The match was played on a Sunday in June, just before the start of the respective northern hemisphere tours. The Leicester side that started against us had seven current England players and we'd only got together a few days before the match.

Leicester scored within two minutes and they would have thought that we had simply pitched up for a week of boozing but this was a Barbarians team packed with brilliant individuals and with some wonderful combinations, which made it that much easier for us to gel. Springboks Os du Randt and Adrian Garvey were my props, the All Blacks Robin Brooke and Ian Jones were at lock and the loose trio was Ruben Kruger, Lawrence Dallaglio and New Zealand's Zinzan Brooke, who had announced it would be his last rugby match.

That is some pack and the backs were also world-class, with Fijian centre Viliame Satala, Fijian-born All Blacks wing Joeli Vidiri and French fullback Thomas Castaignede sensational on the day. We scored 13 tries to Leicester's one and embarrassed England's finest club side 81-10. It remains the heaviest defeat in Leicester's history. I scored a try and, for one day in 2000, I again felt like a rugby player who was the world's best in his position.

It was good to be among such fantastic players and to be celebrated as one of those fantastic players, but it didn't change Nick Mallett's mind about me and the Springboks. He had written me off after the 1998 end-of-year tour, had not picked me in 1999 and showed no interest in me in 2000.

Reality returned very quickly when I got back to Johannesburg from London. I had no appetite for Mains and didn't want to be part of his team. Mains had an agenda at the Lions and it was to get rid of Doc Louis Luyt. He also had an ally in Hennie le Roux, who hated Doc Luyt and wanted to see him gone.

Mains and Hennie were trying to get the players to turn against Doc Luyt and I publicly challenged Mains in front of all the players. He got aggressive with me and told me to shut up. I told him to shut up and reminded him he was a foreigner in our country. I told him he always had an escape of going back to New Zealand if his plan failed but the young players in the team would be left behind to deal with the mess. I asked him what would happen to them if they turned against Doc Luyt, weren't successful and then got fired. Would Mains pay their salaries? Mains said I was an informer to Doc Luyt and he tried to turn the team against me.

He was petty and childish. At one training session he switched me to the so-called B team and gave instructions to the A-team to rough me up and humiliate me. It was the first and last time he tried that because when it came to roughing up, I was the one dishing it out at training.

Mains had very few A-grade personality traits and he was a miserable fuck. I hated playing rugby when Mains was at Ellis Park and it made it that much easier to justify why my personal life was in free fall.

Shortly before the liquidation of my chemical business, the owners of a local family business - a father, mother and son team - came to my offices without invitation and without the liquidator. I asked them to leave the premises and they swore at me. The son, who was a lot bigger than me, bumped me on the way out and threatened me. I told them all to piss off and went back up to my office. The more I thought about how they had insulted me the angrier I became. I went back downstairs and the three were still in the car park. When I walked outside the son insulted my sister with the most disgusting profanity. I may not have a close relationship with my sister but she is my sister and no one speaks about my sister like that. No one speaks about a woman the way he did and I told him he was going to pay for it. I confronted them and, while the son and I were arguing, the mother hit me over the head with a torch. It split my forehead and then I punched her son. She ran to the car and the husband was running away. I told him he would be next if they didn't get off my premises.

They made an assault case and after several court appearances, with varying accounts and a magistrate who made it clear she was going to make an example of me, my lawyer advised me to plead guilty and take a R5000 fine. It is the only time I have ever been convicted of any criminal charge in my life and it couldn't have come at a worse time.

My head was fucked. I was running on fumes and running on empty. I was mixing with characters that I would not be mixing with today. I had been at the height of my international rugby career and I had abandoned it all.

It was just one destruction after the other and this continuous dark trend in my life. I couldn't break the momentum and when I look back on that time all I think is, "how the hell did I land up there?"

THROWN A RUGBY LIFELINE

Andrea and I started talking more regularly in 2000. We were friends and even though there was this instant connection and attraction, our initial chats were more casual and not about our feelings towards each other. She didn't deny the chemistry was there but it wasn't necessary for either of us to unpack the attraction. I enjoyed interacting with her and found relief in her being older and 'having lived'.

I was also coming to terms with Julio's death and just how my life was in free fall. I had to start asking the hard questions because I just couldn't continue destroying myself. I had missed out on so many inspiring things in 1999 and 2000, most notably the chance of playing in the Rugby World Cup.

I was starting to miss rugby even if I wasn't yet at the stage where I could admit it to myself but what I did know was that the intrigue of the Hells Angels had subsided and I needed to get away from Peter Conway. I was sick and tired of the monotony of the lifestyle, of the boozing, recreational drug use and available working women. I was tired of Conway and more and more I was seeing him as a con artist instead of as a rebel without a cause. He very much had a cause and it was tied into working with the National Intelligence and doubling as an informer to the police. He wasn't what he presented to the underworld and I owed my dad an apology because he had warned me from the moment Conway and I started becoming friends.

My lifestyle choices were not only ruining me but also my closest friendships. Camillo was no longer sharing my house and we were only starting to talk again after a fall out that was brought on by my behaviour. Andrea and I had started to take the friendship a bit further to include dinners and a few dates. I enjoyed having a woman in my life again, even though I knew the shadow of Shelley loomed large. In our conversations, I had opened up to Andrea about Shelley and my broken heart so there was no secret as to the mental state I was in when it came to love and to having a girlfriend.

Andrea and I started spending more and more time together and slowly the sanity started to return to my days. The more time with Andrea meant less time with Conway and Angels. I only played a handful of matches for the Lions in 2000, and I knew there was no future for me at the union while Laurie Mains was coaching. I also wasn't convinced that I wanted a future in rugby any more. I questioned whether my time had come and gone. Andrea wasn't as sure as I thought I was and she started challenging me about my premature walking away from rugby. She asked questions about my glory days and made me think about being a Springbok. She wanted to know what my best rugby memory was and she took an interest in why I had loved the game and what I felt I had given to the game and got back from it.

She triggered positive memories about the word "rugby" and not the negative ones that came with Laurie Mains. She encouraged me to start training, if not for rugby, then to get fit and to feel good about myself. My physical shape and conditioning had been important to me since high school, I liked to look good and I got great confidence from being in shape.

Then Carlo got assassinated, shot in the back while standing next to me at his car outside the Gecko Lounge in Johannesburg. I had already lost Julio to bullets and Carlo's death was one loss too many.

I had nowhere to turn but rugby, and a chance lunch meeting with former Bok prop and businessman Guy Kebble would be the catalyst that eventually got me back on the field. Guy had invested in the Falcons Rugby Union and he wanted me to play for the Falcons. He said he had big plans for the province and wanted to show that a small union could be successful professionally if run by the right business people. He said he needed a marquee signing and a player who understood the people from the area and who could lead from the front. He said I fitted the bill perfectly. I'd known Brett Kebble for a while and, even though I liked Guy's brother, I had considered him a bit of a "Bullshit Bertie". I told Guy that I would come captain his Falcons team but I wanted to be paid R50 000 a month. I added a few more extras and benefits during our chat thinking that nothing would come from it. We settled into a lunch drinking session and the merrier Guy became, the bigger his dream with the Falcons sounded.

We shook hands, I gave him my number and told him to call me to sort out the details.

And then he called a few days later. I was stunned as it was the last thing I expected.

He said the R50 000 a month had been sorted, which was thanks to his father Roger Kebble, and he needed me at Falcons training.

Andrea was as surprised as I was at the news. I wasn't in the best shape but I had already started to train and I'd also signed up a personal trainer to well and truly stuff me up and take me back to a place of physical pain that comes from pushing your body.

My rugby success had come because I looked after my body and conditioned it to take the beatings that come in a contact sport. I had also been fortunate with injury for most of my career and the only time I suffered serious injury, at the start of 1999, was because I was out of shape, arrogant in my attitude and believing that I could leg press 500 kilograms without having been in a gym for a month. A torn groin was the result of me acting like King Kong and being stupid.

If I was going to do this rugby thing again, I had to do it properly. I wasn't going to the Falcons to embarrass myself, I was going there to reinvent James Dalton and crucially I was going there to get back my love for playing rugby.

2002: NOT A GREAT VINTAGE

I finally settled back into rugby in 2001 and it meant my life started to settle down, too. Phil Pretorius was the coach of the Falcons and he was also the Bulls Super Rugby coach. He was just a uniquely odd character, whose ideas of rugby left me bemused. Peter de Villiers, who would coach the Springboks from 2008 to 2011, was his assistant. The two were lost as a coaching combination and I can't say I found my game enriched through their coaching.

But I was starting to enjoy being on a rugby field again and while my initial return was to play for the Falcons, I was asked to make myself available for the Bulls in Super Rugby. I did and in 2001 and 2002 I played a total of 16 matches for the Bulls and even captained them a few times. I also got through 18 matches for the Falcons and where 2001 was all about proving a point to myself, 2002 was about wanting to wear the green and gold jersey.

It troubled me that I hadn't left Springbok rugby on my terms at the end of 1998. In 35 Test matches for South Africa between 1994 and 1998 I'd only lost three, and I'd only ever played in one losing Bok Test at home during that time, and that was the 33-26 defeat to the All Blacks in Pretoria in 1996. I hungered for more Test matches and my thinking had transformed from the dark place I found myself in during 1999 and 2000.

Rugby was feeling easy for me because I was in such good shape. I was fit and conditioned and my trials and tribulations had humbled me. I took nothing for granted when it came to rugby. I wanted to be the best again and in 2002 I felt my form was the best of the SA's Super Rugby and provincial hookers. I had an edge to my game and I had solace in my private life. There was a rhythm and structure to my day. Rugby was the dominant motivator when I got up every morning and I dared to start dreaming of wearing that Springboks jersey again.

My craving to play Test rugby was similar to wanting to make the 1995 Rugby World Cup squad. I was enthusiastic about life and I had my strut back. Rudolf Straeuli, my old teammate at Transvaal and with the Springboks in 1994 and 1995, had been appointed Springbok coach in 2002 and he had contacted me to sound me out and get an understanding of my head space. He told me he had been impressed with my Super Rugby form and wanted to know my appetite for Test rugby. It was a pleasant exchange and I said I was back in the game to play international rugby. I reassured him that I could be an asset to any Bok squad and that I was in the best shape of my life.

Rudolf's interest in me added to my motivation in the final few weeks of Super Rugby and I knew I had played myself into contention for a Springbok recall four years after the low of losing to England at Twickenham.

I was like a kid in a candy store because I'd worked so hard in 2001 and 2002 to put myself in this position. I had tested myself against everyone in South African Super Rugby and didn't consider any of the new generation of hooker to be in the same class of those I had played against internationally between 1994 and 1998. Rudolf rated Sharks hooker Lukas van Biljon, but while Lucas had fire and brimstone in his belly, he was raw and unrefined. He was a tough competitor, and I actually came to enjoy his company, but there were so many limitations to his skill set and when Lukas couldn't dominate physically, he didn't offer much more.

I had made it clear to Rudolf that if I came into the Springbok squad, it would be to show I was the best and to play. I would impart whatever knowledge I had and hope to inspire the younger players but I didn't want to be selected to be a mentor who would play second fiddle because of my age. I wanted to be picked because he rated me as first choice.

Rudolf said he wanted me there to be a leader and to take charge of the front row and it remains a career highlight when I was selected to start against Wales in Bloemfontein in 2002. I felt such pride that I had got myself out of the gutter and worked my arse off to be considered the country's best in my position. I was grateful for the support of Andrea and Camillo and inspired by the memory of Julio and Carlo. I knew how precious these moments were and how easily they disappeared. It was a proud day for my dad to see how his son had got up off the canvas to fight back.

I was in a disciplined state of mind when I arrived at my first Bok training session in four years. Rudolf had decided the squad would live at the Pretoria Police College and my first experience of him as a coach was so different to the guy who was my teammate for so long at Transvaal.

Rudolf's charm as a player was his naughtiness and ability to be the joker. He had a dry sense of humour and was always at the forefront of any team prank. He was fun to be around as a player but he wasn't fun to have around as a coach.

The idea to take the squad to the Police College was just nonsense and it was evident from the first day that Rudolf, instead of being his own man, was trying to be Kitch Christie. Kitch was a senior statesman of the game and had earned the right to be who he was as a coach. Rudolf was still an apprentice coach and he misread the year and how the game and players had evolved. The game was now professional and if you expected players to behave like professionals then you needed to treat them like professionals.

Rudolf had this obsession with wanting to take players out of their comfort zones but he was misguided with what he thought was a comfort zone or an uncomfortable zone. Locking players behind the gates of the Police College and treating them like student constables was not going to make them better rugby players.

Rudolf tried to apply the training principles used by Kitch in 1995 and the same attitude as a coach towards his players. It was all wrong and it made for the weirdest of national training camps. I couldn't wait to get out of the Police College and get stuck into some Test action. I also found it strange to have Rudolf as the Bok coach, and as the guy coaching me.

All my memories in rugby of Rudolf were as a player and while I wanted to show him respect as an international coach, it was a respect that had to be earned. He wasn't going to do it being paranoid and cynical. He certainly wasn't going to do it by spying on players and constantly doubting the motives of players. And he also wasn't going to do it through ongoing power-play games with players.

South African rugby, in 2002, lacked the international depth and class of player that had been available between 1995 and 2000. I had played in sides with some of the greatest Springboks and players who were the best in the world. I was privileged to be in the 1995 and 1997/1998 Bok teams and if I took the quality of player for granted back then, I didn't need a second training session to know how little quality there was in the 2002 squad.

I had scrummed down with Balie Swart as my tighthead prop in 1995 and Adrian Garvey in 1998. My locks in 1995 and 1998 were Mark Andrews, Hannes Strydom and Krynauw Otto. Now I had Lawrence Sephaka on my right and Hottie Louw and Jannes Labuschagne behind me. With the greatest respect to Hottie, Jannes and Lawrence, they just couldn't compare or compete.

A handful of the younger players from 2002 would become exceptional Springboks, with lock Bakkies Botha the most significant. Joe van Niekerk would also play more than 50 Tests and be considered one of the best in the game, but the rest were a combination of players just not good enough or consistent enough for Test rugby. Bobby Skinstad was one of the appointed leaders but he was never the same player after damaging his knee in a car accident in 1999. Corne Krige captained the side and you couldn't fault Corne for courage or commitment, but he was not in the class of Francois Pienaar and Gary Teichmann.

Rudolf always seemed to be conflicted when it came to selections. He picked Bobby but always gave me the impression he did it grudgingly. And he talked up Corne as a captain and player but in a way that made me doubt whether he believed what he was saying.

While it was a very different Springbok change room to the one I had been in at the end of 1998, the lure of the jersey was exactly the same. It was an emotional moment getting that Test jersey for the first time in four years. I felt like I had been given a second chance, which is something Carlo wasn't given when gunmen pumped so many bullets into his body. When I was given that Test jersey, I held it as tightly as I had done Carlo's dying body. I gave thanks to him as a friend and, in my mind, dedicated my first Test back to him and Julio. This was an occasion bigger than just a rugby match. Emotionally I was charged up because I was going to be playing for much more than just myself.

It was a Test that I was determined wouldn't be lost and never did I think we would lose the Test or the series. There is something unique about playing for the Springboks in South Africa because it doesn't matter how vulnerable or weak a Springbok team may be, there is always this belief within the squad and among supporters that the Boks win at home.

It is certainly all I knew as my only taste of defeat was coming on with 15 minutes to play against the All Blacks at Loftus Versfeld in 1996 and losing 33-26. That All Blacks team was one of the greatest but we always believed we would beat them, and when we didn't it shocked us.

Some would call it arrogance but there is a remarkable confidence among Springbok players in Tests at home. The Boks set-up in 2002 was inferior to the one I had left behind in 1998, but one thing didn't change: we won at home. On 8 June, 2002, we clubbed Wales 34-19 and the next weekend we grinded out a 19-8 win at a wet Newlands.

The Welsh typically spoke a bigger game than they ended up playing. Rudolf had asked me to silence their hooker, Robin McBryde. He arrived in South Africa with a reputation as the strong man of their pack but he left Newlands with two closed eyes and not a hell of a lot to say.

Rudolf thanked me for my professionalism and attitude within the team after the series win and I felt it wasn't my place to tell him what I thought he was getting wrong as a coach. I didn't want him to think I still saw him as a teammate who could say whatever I wanted to. I had to keep the distance between the two of us and not let the familiarity of our playing days create any grey area.

Perhaps I got it wrong by saying nothing, but I don't think it would have changed his approach. He was very dogmatic and singular in how he saw things in 2002 and it wasn't very inspiring.

STRAEULI A BIG LETDOWN

Ellis Park has always been a spiritual home to me when it comes to the Springboks. I was wearing the No 2 jersey when we beat the All Blacks there in 1996, and again at the same venue the following year in the win against the British and Irish Lions. In 1998, we beat Australia at Ellis Park to claim our first Tri Nations title, and four years later I'd play my last home Test there in a 33-31 win against the then world champions Australia.

I never lost a Test match at Ellis Park and in 20 Tests in South Africa, would only be on the losing side twice. Both of those Tests were to the All Blacks, in Pretoria in 1996 and in Durban in 2002.

The 2002 season had started with a series victory against Wales and a one-off Test win against Argentina in Springs. It was cool to be part of a Test at the PAM Brink Stadium in Springs because of the Falcons connection and it was also very cool to play one more time against my old foe Federico Mendez, who I rated as one of the best.

I'd play Mendez four times in Test rugby and he was always a tough customer. He was big and physical and could scrum. He was also a good man and what happened on the field, stayed on the field. He wasn't a dirty player and there wasn't much off-the-ball stuff with him. He just focused on using his 30-kilogram weight advantage to wear opponents down in the scrum. I rated him and I liked him.

Argentina had never beaten the Springboks and while it was always a bruising match, we had too much skill back then to ever be beaten. Even with a Springboks team considered young, inexperienced and vulnerable, we'd still put 49 points past them.

The Springs win was the third in succession and meant that I had lost just once in my last 21 Tests. I should have driven home after that match and never returned because there was to be very little to celebrate with the Boks for the rest of the year.

I played for a team that lost more Tests in the next few months than I had lost in my entire international career. We were smashed in six of the season's last seven Test matches, with the only respite again coming at Ellis Park.

I loved that ground and somehow never doubted we were unbeatable when playing there. I don't know what it was but I felt invincible when running out of that tunnel. Clearly, so did those guys I played alongside because we always won our Test matches at Ellis Park.

The win against Australia in 2002 would be the last time I'd play a Test in South Africa. It was an incredible match because we started brilliantly and then Australia showed all their class to hit back in the second half and turn a 26-9 deficit into a 31-26 lead with a few minutes to go.

Australia had some fantastic players and they could score tries but it would have been embarrassing to lose at home after leading 26-9. I played the first 60 minutes and when I left the field we were still in the lead and were expected to finish them off in the last 20 because of altitude and superior conditioning. The opposite happened - they got stronger, we buckled and wave after wave of attack resulted in them scoring two tries.

Brent Russell, playing at flyhalf, and flanker Joe van Niekerk scored great tries but there wasn't a Springboks highlights reel in the second half. It was difficult to watch the final 20 minutes from the sideline but fortunately the bounce of the ball favoured us in the last couple of minutes and Bolla Conradie and Werner Greeff combined for a great try. Werner then nailed the winning conversion. Ellis Park, as a ground, had again produced a Test victory, although it was only just.

We had avoided being whitewashed after losing to the Wallabies and All Blacks overseas and to the All Blacks in Durban but even then, there was a reluctance from Rudolf to allow the team to celebrate.

Any Test win is a good one and when you beat the world champions, stay in the moment, pat yourself on the back and hit the town. I did encourage the boys to do that at our team court session. I also made them aware of where to party and where not to because they would be a target for that one idiot who wanted to make a name for himself.

There had been an issue with Bobby Skinstad, who had been involved in a fight in a Johannesburg nightclub a few months earlier. He had attacked Peter Lindenberg, a well-known powerboat racing champion, after Lindenberg and Skinstad's brother had been in a fight. Peter was connected and, on request from Rudolf, I needed to tap into my connections to ensure there wasn't retaliation and revenge against Bobby or any of the Springboks.

My relationship with Andrea and my rugby comeback had made for a calmer me and I wasn't playing in the nightclub space, but after beating Australia I wanted to celebrate.

Andrea would be at my side when I left the team hotel on Saturday evening and I knew that all the players had to be back for a ridiculous 7am flush-out session on Sunday morning. These Sunday morning sessions were more Rudolf trying to be Kitch Christie than anything else. We were also expected to attend a birthday breakfast for South African Rugby Union President Silas Nkanunu at the Montecasino team hotel. The players didn't care much for the breakfast but Rudolf had insisted everyone be present.

Our Tri Nations campaign was over and as the Saturday night progressed, I didn't see the sense in anything that had been arranged for Sunday. I wanted to be with Andrea and my mates and I wanted to sleep at home in my own bed. We'd been on the road for a month and I was drained from Rudolf's conspiracy theories and the militant-type team environment. I am sure the rest of the players felt the same.

I never made it back to the team hotel for the 7am swimming session. Instead I was cuddled up in my bed at my home. I was prepared to suffer whatever consequence would come from breaking protocols that were absurd in the context of the night.

It had been a long and testing month and the overseas Tests had been a disaster. We were hammered in both Tests and Rudolf's paranoia had been on high alert in Brisbane and Wellington. His selections had been questionable and the entire fortnight had been difficult. I knew we had no chance of winning the two Tests because we weren't good enough as a team.

The last time I'd been in Wellington with the Springboks was in 1998 and we'd won 13-3. This time I was there with decidedly inferior teammates and there would be no cause for celebration in a 41-20 defeat. I wasn't used to playing in a Bok team that conceded 40 points and I had seldom played in Test defeats. What made the result worse was we led 13-0 after 10 minutes, so you don't have to imagine how the last 70 minutes played out.

The match against Australia the following week was just as disappointing, if not as emphatic. It was the first time I'd play at the Gabba Cricket Ground, but the size and formation of the pitch made it feel very strange. The crowd was always very far from the field and it was a match that seemed to lack in intensity and atmosphere. There was a free-for-all fight and the Australian wing Ben Tune ended up blindsiding Corne Krige with a punch and De Wet Barry returned to the change room with one of George Smith's dreadlocks. It wasn't a memorable Test, but it was the first time in my international career that I'd experience successive Test losses.

South Africa had won the first four Tests of the year and Rudolf battled to cope with the back-to-back defeats. There was some comfort for him being back at Kings Park for the All Blacks Test because he lived in Durban but the pressure of losing and his inexperience as a Test coach were making him even more paranoid.

I couldn't relate to him and tried to keep my focus on my performance, my attitude and my positivity but it was a foreign experience being with the Boks in 2002, when I compared it to my Test career between 1994 and 2002. So much had changed and I found everything to be politically correct, sanitised and soft. This Bok squad also didn't command presence and they never owned the field. They were from a different era in every sense of the word when I compared them to the 1995 World Cup winners.

The players lacked mongrel and they also didn't have the class of their predecessors. I didn't have a lot of faith in them but I backed the South African factor to be decisive in giving us an edge against the All Blacks, who were also struggling for quality in certain positions, most notably hooker and lock.

Piet van Zyl, some fat bastard supporter who thought he was doing us a favour in the first half, got onto the field and tackled Irish referee Dave McHugh. Ordinarily, I'd have had no objection because it was McHugh who had red-carded me at the 1995 World Cup, but we were winning the Test when this village idiot took him out of the match, and the incident stopped our momentum.

The All Blacks, as they so often do, produced a late moment of magic and won the Test and now it was three Boks defeat in succession.

Players will tell you there are occasions when your reputation is enhanced through absence and by the end of 2002, I had come to know what they meant.

The win against Australia gave us some relief and some good press but it hadn't given Rudolf enough confidence because by the time he announced a weakened squad to play against France, Scotland and England, he was a mess.

Whatever his reasons for resting players, he had to have known that this was a tour that could only have a bad ending. We'd struggled enough in the Tri Nations when supposedly at full strength and now we were going to play an in-form England at Twickenham with this lot?

I prepared myself for the worst but no one could have prepared us for what was to come.

It was another Bok tour of firsts for me. I'd never lost to France before getting on a plane to Paris in November of 2002, and I'd also never known the kind of embarrassment and humiliation that was awaiting us in Edinburgh and London.

Never did I think of pulling out of the tour. I'd spent four years away from Test rugby and had missed it. I was grateful for every opportunity I now got to wear the Bok jersey and every time I played, I wanted to honour my mates Carlo and Julio.

I'd like to think I put my body on the line in Marseilles and at Twickenham but we were just not good enough with a touring squad of players who in another era would have struggled to make a good club side.

It also didn't help that Rudolf changed the team strategy on the day of the match against France and that our players were so ill-prepared mentally for the atmosphere at the stadium in Marseilles. We'd prepared all week at a golf resort about an hour outside of Marseilles and we were totally disconnected from the occasion. The mentality of the Marseilles crowd was one of aggression and crassness and the French players thrived on this energy. Our guys didn't know what had hit them. When there's a lot of false bravado in the change room before kick-off, and players uncharacteristically screaming to hype themselves up, you know they're shitting themselves.

It was a terrible night and we got physically beaten up in every legal way. I was playing for South Africa again, but in my heart I knew this wasn't a team of players who should be calling themselves Springboks.

Rudolf didn't know how to handle the defeat in Marseilles and he had lost the respect of the players even before we left France for Scotland. He had kept the players up till 2am on the Sunday with a match review and then forced the team to have a traditional court session. It was impossible to be enthusiastic at 3am in the morning, but in Rudolf's mind we were bonding and adversity was apparently going to make us stronger. It didn't.

Rudolf had told me before the tour that I would play France and England and Lukas van Biljon would start against Scotland, but everything he said after the defeat in Marseilles was a contradiction of what he had said before leaving South Africa.

It got crazy and all week in Edinburgh he played mind games with the players. He didn't want to announce the team until the latest possible time and he wouldn't tell anyone who was starting until the Thursday. There were contact sessions when recovery should have been a priority and he only finalised the reserves after an early evening scrumming machine session on the Friday before the Test.

You couldn't make up this stuff but he even starved the players of water during the training sessions to teach them some sort of lesson from the French defeat.

I had been on Super Rugby tours before when the wheels came off but never had I known a Springbok tour to so quickly spiral into free fall.

Scotland destroyed South Africa 21-6 and I sat on the bench, all dressed up and with nowhere to go or hide. It was a disgraceful performance and I was grateful I didn't get on because I didn't want to be associated with such a gutless effort from the Boks. I was livid watching and I'd discover later that evening just how livid the South African supporters were who had paid to be at Murrayfield.

Rudolf didn't want the players to go out after Murrayfield because he knew there would be trouble. He told the players he had already been verbally abused on the way to the change room and the bus and that it would be even worse at the bars and the nightclubs.

The players didn't care and they wanted to go out. I saved Lukas van Biljon from having to explain his evening and spent the early part of the night putting out more fires than I have ever started.

This was one night when we had to take it on the chin from supporters because they had every right to be angry and the players' only escape was to drink in the hope of momentarily forgetting the day had ever happened.

But it did and when the sun came up on the Sunday, the new day only reinforced the horror of Saturday and the potential horror of what would be waiting for us at Twickenham.

Rudolf, in another of those brain explosions, had decided the squad would travel from Edinburgh to London by train, alongside thousands of South Africans who had travelled up from London.

The mood of the supporters hadn't eased off overnight and they were abusive towards us at the station. There had also been a mix-up in the train booked for us and our train would take five hours to get to London. Many of the younger players didn't seem to be as bothered by the result of the match and were way too cheerful for my liking. I reminded them of how *kak* they had been by reading out loud some of the player rankings in the Scottish Newspapers. Some players had been given a three out of 10 and I let them know it should have been one out of 10.

England, who would win the World Cup in 2003, had beaten

the All Blacks in New Zealand and had also beaten the Wallabies in Australia earlier in the year. They were a powerhouse team, with an outstanding captain in Martin Johnson and one of the game's best ever flyhalves in Jonny Wilkinson.

I didn't need to study their team line-up to know we were in trouble because I simply had to look at ours at training.

I had played England at Twickenham three times, in 1995, 1997 and 1998. We had won easily in 1995 and 1997 and lost our unbeaten run in 1998. My rugby memories were good ones whenever I was in London and I loved the hype that an England versus Springboks showdown generated in the media.

But this time it was different because the outcome of the match was a certainty. The English media knew it and they seemed half apologetic in having to conduct interviews with us. When I had been in London in 1995 and 1997 you could sense the nervousness of the England players through the attitude of the British media. In 2002 there was no nervousness because there was nothing to be nervous about.

Rudolf, knowing that the team he would send to battle wasn't a good enough rugby team, turned the build-up into a frenzy of physicality. He wanted us to go at each other in training and be physically imposing. It was a case of hit first before getting hit.

England's captain Martin Johnson was an obvious target. He was their leader and their strongman and Rudolf felt that if he had to take a step back, then so would the rest of the players. Matt Dawson, the scrumhalf, and Wilkinson were also names that cropped up all week.

It was all hot air and just words because when I looked around it was clear we didn't have the players who could make a physical statement and we didn't have the players who could make a rugby statement.

For the first time in my Test career I knew I was taking the field and that we were going to take a beating in the collisions, in the set piece and on the scoreboard. I wasn't going to concede anything individually but there was no collective to support the effort.

Rudolf had got into the head of lock Jannes Labuschagne, who was a nice guy and not much more than a rugby journeyman. Jannes was more dependable than dynamic as a lock and he was more pacifier than pitbull. I don't know how Rudolf expected him to change his nature and all that the pre-match screaming did was confuse Jannes, who so uncharacteristically threatened Johnson after the playing of the national anthems. The poor guy was out of control mentally and the disintegration happened within the first 20 minutes when he was shown a red card for the clumsiest of late tackles on Wilkinson.

We were down to 14 men against the best team in the world, who were playing at home. If the referee had any mercy, he would have stopped the Test the moment 14 had to play 15 because even when it was 15 versus 15, it was a mismatch.

The match descended into a mess where every Springbok player seemed to be doing his own thing. A lot of blows were thrown by both sides, although any English punches, late hits or knees to the back hardly rated a mention because of the score.

England won 53-3, but what dominated the match review was allegations of Bok thuggery. Johnson and England coach Clive Woodward described us as a disgrace to world rugby. Corne Krige, as captain, took the brunt of the criticism and they described his fighting as "five minutes of madness".

Rudolf was crushed afterwards. I've never seen the big guy look so small as he tried to talk to the players in the change room. This was the darkest day in Springbok rugby history and there was nowhere to run or hide. There was no escaping the result and there would be no let-up of the accusations of foul play.

We were told afterwards that Woodward had convinced the Rugby Football Union to install cameras all around the ground to help with capturing of statistical player data, and these cameras were in addition to the broadcaster's cameras. Every ruck had been captured and every collision was on camera, and it was based on this that Woodward accused us of premeditated madness.

He then produced the evidence and it read like this:

3rd minute: Robinson punched by Krige after late tackle.
10th minute: Dalton punches Dawson.
12th minute: Fleck punches Cohen.
20th minute: Robinson hit off the ball by James.
21st minute: Dawson complains to ref of Bok cheap shots.
23rd minute: Labuschagne sent off for late shoulder charge on Wilkinson.
35th minute: Krige is penalised for late hit on Hill.
40th minute: James punches Dawson.
41st minute: Wilkinson out of game after James shoulder charge.
50th minute: Greeff knees Back from the side.
55th minute: Krige headbutts Dawson.
58th minute: Krige knocked out Pretorius in charging for Dawson, who ducks a stiff arm.
61st minute: Greeff concedes penalty-try with dangerous tackle on Christophers.
69th minute: Krige elbows Johnson.
74th minute: Venter headbutts Hill in the face.

Rudolf's response was to tell the English media to go look at the scenes in the Bok change room.

"How do you explain my change room?" he asked. "I have two players concussed. Do you think we knock out our own players?"

The answer was that we do because, as video evidence later showed, Corne had swung a punch at England's Dawson, who had ducked as Andre Pretorius went in for the tackle on Dawson. Corne's punch broke Pretorius' nose and knocked him cold.

It was the ultimate humiliation for Rudolf as the coach. There was nothing to say. The rugby year was done and as I looked around the change room I knew that most of those players' international careers were done.

Rudolf insisted on holding the traditional team court session on the Saturday evening but it was as misguided a decision as any he had made on the tour.

The players weren't interested and there could be no celebration of anything when you've just lost by 50 points.

I couldn't wait to get out of the hotel and meet up with a few friends in London. I didn't need any more reminding of the match and my mates wouldn't be talking rugby to me.

I had an hour to kill before meeting them in the city centre and there was a place opposite our team hotel in Kensington High Street that looked festive. I walked across with one of the team management members to have a drink but when we got there the bouncer wanted us to queue.

I hadn't queued since I was in high school and I wasn't going to start in London on the night we took 50 points from England. The doorman was tall and had the look of a man confident he could handle himself. I walked up to him and asked him who did his medical aid?

He smiled and said the cover cost was 10 pounds.

I said that we clearly had established there would be no need to queue but now we had to get an understanding that there would be no cover charge.

He looked at me and said: "If you guys hadn't played like such cunts, I'd have let you in for free, so let's settle on five pounds."

He had a point. We had played like cunts and I duly paid the five pounds entrance fee.

HANGING UP MY BOK BLAZER

The England Test bugged me throughout the summer of 2003. I knew we were never good enough to beat England but I never imagined being in a Springboks team that would be beaten by 50 points at Twickenham.

The result was disgusting but the team performance was as ugly to have experienced and to have witnessed, if you were a fan.

What I couldn't accept was how little it seemed to mean to so many of the squad. There was no hurt in the embarrassment and there was no respect for the Springbok jersey.

Rudolf (Straeuli) as Springbok coach was in denial about the tour and all I heard was excuse after excuse about our defeats. There was no honest assessment and Rudolf just wasn't coping as the Springboks coach.

I'd always arrived in London to play England with a strut and with my chest puffed out, but in 2002 we had arrived by train from Edinburgh, almost apologetically for being there.

I'd left Twickenham in 1998 disappointed at my own performance, but knowing I was broken and we, as a unit, were physically exhausted and mentally drained after 17 successive Test wins. I wouldn't play Test rugby again for four years, but when I made my international comeback in 2002 against Wales in Bloemfontein, I didn't think the year would end with a 53-3 defeat against England.

I once again left Twickenham a broken player, but this time it had nothing to do with fatigue.

I was fed up with what the Springboks had become. They were a joke to the world and there was no respect for them on the end of season tour. The French mocked us, Scotland hammered us and England completely disregarded us.

The tour shamed the Springboks, in results, in discipline and in overall effort, and I didn't buy into the public relations talk that we were a team building for the 2003 World Cup.

I'd played in the 1995 World Cup, missed out on going to the 1999 World Cup and had never given 2003 a thought back in 2000 and 2001. It was only when I started playing Test rugby again in 2002 that the prospect of making it to 2003 became real and when we won our first four Tests of 2002 the fire burned within me. I wanted to make a difference for the Springboks and was willing to make any sacrifice. I was in great physical shape and felt I was the best hooker in South Africa. I also hadn't faced any international hooker that was in the class of New Zealand's Sean Fitzpatrick, even though I still enjoyed my final showdown at Springs in 2002 with Argentina's Federico Mendez.

The Mendez challenge and the passion belonged in 2002 and, when 2003 arrived, I just couldn't find that fire to go to the World Cup. I tried to convince myself that it was what I wanted but my attitude towards the Cats and Super Rugby didn't speak to any desire to be part of the Springboks 2003 World Cup squad.

I dug deep into my consciousness in the early part of the season, maybe to prove something to myself, but as hard as I trained physically, mentally I just wasn't there in 2003.

Bobby Skinstad was captaining the Cats and Tim Lane was the coach. Tim was a good bloke, who had played for Australia, been an assistant coach to the 1999 World Cup-winning Wallabies and been Rudolf Straeuli's Springboks assistant in 2002. Tim rated me, got on with me and backed me, but I just couldn't give the

Cats leadership the James Dalton they wanted as an investment.

Rugby, which was so important to me in 2002, was now an afterthought and it came to a head early in the 2003 Super Rugby season when Bobby phoned me to ask me why I wasn't at a Sunday evening team video session.

I happened to be at a DVD store with Andrea when Bobby called and I told him I didn't even know there was a team session. It was then that I knew I was doing myself a disservice and I was doing the Cats an even bigger disservice if I continued to be a part of the squad when mentally I was so detached from rugby.

The game of rugby, since I was 14 years old, had been my everything. I owned the rugby field at Jeppe and wherever I played in the world I felt I was in charge when I ran onto a field.

The great irony is that mentally I was in such a stable place in 2003 but from a rugby perspective, the 2002 end of year tour had finished me.

I had played Test rugby against the best hookers of my generation in New Zealand's Sean Fitzpatrick (three times), Ireland's Keith Wood (three times), Australia's Phil Kearns (three times) and big Freddie Mendez (four times). The legendary Uli Schmidt had been a teammate and I'd been part of the two most successful Springbok teams since our return to international rugby in 1992. I had played 20 Test matches at home and only ever lost twice to the All Blacks. I had played 43 Tests, won 35 of them and played 58 matches for the Springboks. I had never lost to eight of the 12 teams I'd played against and before 2002 had never lost to Australia or France. I'd played Test rugby against 15 international hookers in 21 cities in South Africa and abroad, and I had played against many more provincially and in Super Rugby at some of the most recognised rugby destinations. My Lions career included 76 matches and there were 18 matches for the Falcons, 16 for the Bulls and eight for the Cats.

The romantic in me always believed the 58 Tests should have

been a 100 but the realist knew early in 2003 that my rugby career was over.

I called a press conference to announce my retirement. It was emotional and I was frank in telling the media I just didn't have the hunger anymore. I was 30 years old.

BETRAYED BY MY WIFE

I got married to Andrea in 2003. Fuck knows why.

I get emotional and I get angry when I think of how our relationship unfolded. Obviously when we got married, I thought it was the right thing to do. I'd never been in a settled long-term relationship and there was a part of me that thought it had to be because of me.

In 1995 I had committed to a woman who would betray me and in 1997 I had fallen in love with a woman who I had betrayed through refusing to end a friendship with the Hell's Angel Peter Conway. These were my only two intense relationships before I met Andrea. I found comfort in Andrea's maturity and in her age. There was a physical intimacy and there was chemistry but there should never have been a marriage.

I tried between 2003 and 2005 to be a husband to a wife. I wanted to give to the relationship but found myself constantly questioning why I was in this relationship. I always wanted children but with Andrea it was never a consideration. I never thought of her as the mother of my child and that should have been a red flag from the beginning.

She inspired me in certain ways but she also played into my ego and insecurity in other ways.

We were good for each other when we met because we were two unhappy individuals who found comfort in the other's vulnerable state but in time we found ourselves to be opposites and what comforted us in the early days became triggers for all our conflict.

We knew each other's vulnerability and so many circumstances would allow for these triggers to be pulled.

The worst of these happened in November 2007, when I woke to the news that Andrea had accused me of attempted murder. I found out through the media that I had apparently attempted to kill my wife.

Attempted murder? Come on!

I have never known anything as absurd because if I had the intention to harm Andrea in any way, it wouldn't have been an attempt. Physically, it would have been an action that I'd be paying for today through a charge, a conviction and a jail sentence.

Our relationship was over when she made the allegation of attempted murder. We were still living together but we were living different lives. We had become opposites in our thinking, our actions and our everything.

Andrea alleged, more through the media than with any conviction in a criminal case, that I had tried to drown her in a bath and smother her with her dress in our Silver Lakes home.

I didn't try and kill Andrea. Honestly, given the breakdown in our relationship, any such thought would not just have been an attempt because if I had wanted to drown her in the bath then I would have been capable physically of doing so.

Andrea and I were in freefall in our relationship and she knew it as well as I did. She didn't want to accept it and knew that it was only a matter of time before I filed for divorce.

Then came the claim, made to the media before she even took it to the police, that I tried to drown her in a bathtub. What followed was one of the most unjust media trials because the headlines screamed 'attempted murder' but the belated police investigation couldn't even find a starting point.

The case would eventually be thrown out of court because

Andrea had refused to co-operate with the Police. She would not attend meetings with investigating officers and she would not furnish the court with statements so that the prosecution could make a case against me.

She had threatened to destroy me in the media when she left our house and that is all she tried to do, and still tries to do. She did all her talking through the media, made it public what she wanted financially in a divorce settlement and even went to the media with claims that I had pushed a firearm to her head, pressed a knife to her throat and given her a black eye. She claimed, again through the media, that I had numerous affairs with women, visited strip clubs, took drugs and did not take responsibility for our pets, which included three large dogs, six cats, a bird and 20 goldfish and koi.

Whatever she could put out in the media, she did, but when the police needed her to verify anything, she was absent.

I fought a losing battle against the South African media, who all my career had always ran with the headline before verifying any validation.

When Andrea eventually did turn the media accusations into a charge with the police, I handed myself over to the Police and asked for the investigation and for the courts to decide on her lunacy.

I had filed for divorce and for an interdict against Andrea but the media reports were that she had filed for a divorce and for an interdict against *me*. She apparently feared for her life but was still coming to my house on a daily basis when I wasn't there and she hated me so much that she still asked me to employ her after our divorce and kept the Dalton surname for five years after our divorce.

Andrea was an opportunist and in recent years she again went to the media claiming to have 'dodged a bullet' because she was in an abusive relationship with me.

It was all media sensation because the court ruling told a very different story. The police investigators were eventually compelled to tell the magistrate that 'the complainant had lost interest in this case or had no grounds to continue with it' when they failed to provide supporting evidence to her initial allegations.

The magistrate Lynn Pillay, in court and as reported in the media, said: 'I cannot understand why it is taking so long to get a supplementary statement'. She said it appeared there was some kind of 'malicious reason' why the complainant's statement was not yet at court and that the court could not ignore the accused's position.

The case was struck off the roll.

Andrea then told the media she would go to the Pretoria High Court to force me to disclose my assets. She was being obstructionist in the divorce proceedings and claiming R50 000 a month maintenance. She also alleged that our living expenses were R150 000 a month and that she was entitled to the standard of living that I had provided for her.

This was all coming from a woman who had gone to the media to say I attempted to kill her, but refused to assist the police in the investigation.

The court ruled that she got R15 000 a month and dismissed all her other claims.

I got a protection order to keep her away from me, yet the media continued to report her story that she was seeking to get a protection order against me. What the media don't report with as much enthusiasm was why the Court refused to advance any of the allegations she made.

LIVING LIFE AFTER RUGBY

After retiring from rugby, I made the odd cameo in a world unknown to me, such as appearing in the TV dance show, *Strictly Come Dancing*. I think I must have rehearsed for 100 hours during the show and it was among the toughest things I ever did. There were even times I found myself dancing on my own, around my pool, to try and master moves that were more difficult to perform than they were to spell.

I will never mock a dancer and all I have is respect for those men and women who know how to use their feet and have an understanding of rhythm and balance.

I learned a lot, got humbled and again ended up laughing at myself a lot.

My separation and subsequent divorce to Andrea would be a strain on me in the early 2000s, as rugby faded from my daily routine. I had to reinvent myself in business and I also found what I thought was love with Sasha.

The highlight of my life, post rugby, was the birth of my son Daniel. What followed, as I documented at the start of the book, was my battle to stay in my son's life. It's been a demanding decade when it comes to my relationship with Daniel and the only thing that has made it manageable has been my bond with my daughter Mila. She is just the most blessed gift and I treasure her in my life every day.

I am also thankful to her mother Claire for being the perfect mother, and also the most accepting and understanding of friends when it comes to our daughter. Never has she used Mila as a pawn and never has Mila been a discussion or an issue when it comes to our relationship. We both take pride in being parents to Mila, just like I take the greatest pride in being Daniel's father.

Cape Town is home to me today, which means I get to see Mila most days and I also am able to spend a lot of time with her in the company of Claire. My regret is the absence of Daniel in my life but perhaps the future will be kind to both of us and we will all get to experience family life as a unit one day.

Rugby remains in my blood, even if my attention now is from a distance. I write a column for *SA Rugby Magazine* and do video and podcast shows on rugby. I speak at functions about South African rugby and I study the game as religiously as I did when I was a player. I am the biggest supporter of the Springboks and I have gone full circle from being a fan to being a player to being a fan again.

I love what my friend and former Springboks teammate Rassie Erasmus has achieved with the team since being appointed in 2018. Rassie has instilled a pride, passion and accountability that was lacking under Allister Coetzee and he is proving to be as good an international coach as he was a player.

I feel proud to be a Springbok and to have worn the same blazer of those players who represented South Africa at the 2019 World Cup.

I admire what Rassie has achieved as a coach. I have so much respect for his rugby acumen and it is fantastic to see good Bok players make the transition to good coaches. Not many have done it and none have done it quite like Rassie. Respect brother!

I dabbled in coaching when I moved to Cape Town. Jerome Booysen, a man I call a friend and a man who has always been good to me, heads up Belhar Rugby Club. Jerome is notorious in the Western Cape for being among the most influential figures in the underworld. So is his brother Colin. I have got to know both of them in my private capacity over the years and I have worked closely with Jerome at Belhar Rugby Club. My experience of Jerome is that of a man who loves his community, is prepared to give back to the community and particularly loves rugby. The stories about him and Colin are plenty and will always be plenty, but then so are the stories about me. So were the stories about my late friends Julio and Carlo. I'll never judge these men on the opinion of others and all I can comment on is my experience of them. You've read about my friendship with Julio and Carlo and the bond between myself and Jerome is, and always has been, rugby.

Jerome asked me to pop in at the Belhar club and have a look at his rugby structures. He asked for an opinion on his coaching staff and the quality of his rugby players. He wanted to know what they could be doing differently and what it would take to be successful.

I observed, commented and, the next thing I knew, I was part of the coaching structure.

I loved my time at Belhar. I met some of the most incredible individuals and I was as inspired as I was humbled.

I was a player who was used to having every luxury in my club, provincial and international career, and had an expectation when it came to a training facility, a rugby field and the game as a profession.

Belhar showed me a different world, where I got to interact with young and older men who turned to rugby as an escape from the harsh day-to-day realities. There were stories of hardship but there were also remarkable stories of success and the men who found themselves on the opposite ends of these stories would unite in the name of Belhar Rugby Club.

The experience taught me so much, as a person and as someone who thought that, because he played at the highest level, he knew and understood the game of rugby.

I never thought I would be a coach because I never thought I would have the temperament for it. It is a very different challenge to being a player.

The biggest adjustment for me was adapting my thinking to the ever-changing laws of the game, which were very different to when I was playing for South Africa. Discipline doesn't change and I found that the men at Belhar initially struggled with the concept of rugby being a team game played by 15 players.

It was an education for me because it is one thing to channel one's own aggression and be responsible for staying on the field, but as a coach you'd have to find a way of keeping 15 players on the field when asking them for passion, aggression and commitment.

I spent two seasons with Belhar and completed my World Rugby Level Two certificate and my BokSmart certificate but I knew that rugby was not going to be what made up my day. It was never all-consuming to me as a player and for me to be a successful coach, it would have to be everything in my day.

I have several business interests and coaching rugby was more of a hobby than it was ever going to be a professional career. Jerome appreciated where my mind was in terms of business and that my heart wasn't exclusively in rugby. There were multiple changes and lots of player movement and I felt it was a relevant time to also move on.

Rugby is in my blood and I can't escape the bonds within rugby and the occasion that was the winning of the 1995 Rugby World Cup in South Africa. It saddens me how little that squad is celebrated and it also saddens me how the individuals have drifted away from each other. It was an incredible achievement and you would think that the magnitude of that success would always ensure a unity among all those players who found common ground in what was achieved collectively.

But it isn't so and I can understand it to a degree because we are all humans before we are rugby players. We may all play for the Springboks and have a common purpose but it doesn't mean we are friends away from the rugby field. I, for one, will never sit at the same fireplace as Hennie le Roux, who was one of the stars of the 1995 World Cup and a teammate of mine provincially and internationally for almost a decade. I always rated Hennie as a wonderful player but I had little time for him as a human being. He was very instrumental in the disconnect between Lions coach Laurie Mains and myself and when we met at the 10-year reunion of the 1995 World Cup win I let him know exactly what I thought of him.

Time, it is said, is a healer and age mellows one, so when I saw Hennie at the funeral for Springboks and World Cup winning right wing, James Small in 2019, I was at least able to greet him, be civil and move on. There was no animosity but there was also no love. I wish it was different, but it isn't.

The 10-year reunion of the 1995 World Cup-winning team was strange because I thought there would be a greater significance to the boys all being in the same room again but the celebration was muted and I found so many players to be guarded, distant and disinterested when it came to each other. The same applied to the 20-year celebration of our success. We spoke about those who had passed but very little else. I couldn't believe these were the same young men who had given so much for the jersey and for their country. We were such a united group of rugby players back in 1995 but 20 years on, we were a bunch of individuals.

I was also disappointed that so few attended James Small's funeral and the same was true a few months later when the iconic Bok left wing Chester Williams died. James was 50 years old and Chester was 49 but I always think of them as 20-somethings who refused to take a step back against All Blacks Jonah Lomu and Jeff Wilson in the 1995 World Cup final.

James and I were closer than Chester and I were and it

appalled me how the media treated James' death and failed to consider his two children.

I wrote a column for *SA Rugby magazine* saying that James should have been celebrated and honoured for the legacy he left in a Springbok jersey and for the inspiration he gave South Africa as a rugby nation. My column read: "It is unfortunate that in the wake of Small's passing, some of the media and public focus was on a report delving into the personal life of a rugby legend, whose off-field antics are in reality none of my or anybody's business and should be detached from the impact he had on the game and the South African rugby public's love for rugby.

"James was likened to myself, a 'misunderstood individual' – perhaps that's a nice way of putting it when we were guilty of silly behaviour – and while there will always be controversy surrounding him *off* the field, he was never a rebel in a team environment. He was a brilliant rugby player, an icon and somebody I considered a dear friend.

"Playing against James meant playing against a six-star performer. He embodied all the qualities you look for in the modern-day wing. He had pace, strength, skill and tenacity, and with James you always knew you had a teammate who was loyal to the core.

"His loyalty transcended rugby, and as a friend he always had time for you. Not only you, but for your family, too. I regret not having made more of an effort to show my appreciation for this and keep in touch, as it choked me up to say goodbye. His passing is a lesson that life is but a heartbeat.

"There is so much negativity at times in our rugby and certainly in our country, so I question why the media would want to add to this when analysing the fall of a brother and an icon? James was somebody who added true value to his country's rugby history and he should be remembered for the brilliant on-field memories and not because of media reports that taint this legacy."

The media in South Africa is cruel and I have spent the past 20 years on the receiving end of the media's bias. All I can ask is that rugby players are allowed to be rugby players and judged for what they do on the rugby field.

I certainly want to be judged for my 43 Tests and 58 matches for the Springboks. It was my profession and it played out in the public eye. I never had an issue with my performance being criticised because I was representing my country and everyone who watched was emotionally invested in the match. I have never understood why my private life and my relationships should be media headlines because while some in the public may find it interesting, it isn't in the public's interest.

I wanted to tell my rugby story because I felt I had a story to tell and I wanted to front the life I've lived while my rugby career played out in the public eye. I don't want you to think of what you've read as an attempt to justify anything I've done but rather as a reflection of what I experienced as a player and as a man.

I hope I've answered questions you may have had.

BOK CAREER AT A GLANCE

JAMES DALTON - 43 TEST MATCHES					
	DATE	TEAMS AND VENUES	SA RESULT	SCORE	REMARKS
1	08/10/1994	South Africa v Argentina - Boet Erasmus Stadium, Port Elizabeth	Won	42-22	Test debut against Argentina replacing Uli Schmidt in the 75th minute.
2	25/05/1995	South Africa v Australia - Newlands, Cape Town	Won	27-18	Starting debut in 1995 RWC Pool match.
3	03/06/1995	South Africa v Canada - Boet Erasmus Stadium, Port Elizabeth	Won	20-0	Starting, but was sent off in 70th minute together with Canadian captain, Gareth Rees and Canadian prop forward, Rod Snow.
4	02/09/1995	South Africa v Wales - Ellis Park, Johannesburg	Won	40-11	
5	12/11/1995	Italy v South Africa - Olympic Stadium, Rome	Won	21-40	Stadio Olimpico
6	18/11/1995	England v South Africa - Twickenham, London	Won	14-24	
-	17/08/1996	South Africa v New Zealand - Kings Park, Durban	Lost	19-23	Unused substitute
7	24/08/1996	South Africa v New Zealand - Loftus Versfeld, Pretoria	Lost	26-33	Replacing Henry Tromp in the 65th minute.
8	31/08/1996	South Africa v New Zealand - Ellis Park, Johannesburg	Won	32-22	
9	09/11/1996	Argentina v South Africa - Ferro Carril Oeste Stadium, Buenos Aires	Won	15-46	
10	16/11/1996	Argentina v South Africa - Ferro Carril Oeste Stadium, Buenos Aires	Won	21-44	Replaced by Henry Tromp in the 70th minute

11	30/11/1996	France v South Africa - Parc Lescure, Bordeaux	Won	12-22	Replaced by Henry Tromp in the 77th minute
12	07/12/1996	France v South Africa - Parc des Princes, Paris	Won	12-13	Scored his first Test try. The only Springbok try in this Test.
13	15/12/1996	Wales v South Africa - Arms Park, Cardiff	Won	20-37	
14	10/06/1997	South Africa v Tonga - Norwich Park Newlands, Cape Town	Won	74-10	Replacing Fritz van Heerden in the 50th minute as hooker with Naka Drotské to flank.
-	21/06/1997	South Africa v British & Irish Lions - Norwich Park Newlands, Cape Town	Lost	16-25	Unused substitute
-	28/06/1997	South Africa v British & Irish Lions - Kings Park, Durban	Lost	15-18	Unused substitute
15	05/07/1997	South Africa v British & Irish Lions - Ellis Park, Johannesburg	Won	35-16	Replaced by Naka Drotské in the 69th minute
-	02/08/1997	Australia v South Africa - Suncorp Stadium, Brisbane	Lost	32-20	Unused substitute
16	09/08/1997	New Zealand v South Africa - Eden Park, Auckland	Lost	55-35	
17	23/08/1997	South Africa v Australia - Loftus Versfeld, Pretoria	Won	61-22	Scored his second Test try. The 62 points by South Africa is the highest score against Australia and the winning margin of 39 the second biggest against Australia.
18	08/11/1997	Italy v South Africa - Stadio Dall'Ara, Bologna	Won	31-62	Stadio Renato Dall'Ara
19	15/11/1997	France v South Africa - Stade Gérland, Lyon	Won	32-36	Scored his third Test try.
20	22/11/1997	France v South Africa - Parc des Princes, Paris	Won	10-52	
21	29/11/1997	England v South Africa - Twickenham, London	Won	11-29	
22	06/12/1997	Scotland v South Africa - Murrayfield, Edinburgh	Won	10-68	

23	13/06/1998	South Africa v Ireland - Free State Stadium, Bloemfontein	Won	37-13	
24	20/06/1998	South Africa v Ireland - Minolta Loftus, Pretoria	Won	33-0	Scored his fourth Test try. Replaced by Naka Drotské in the 64th minute
25	27/06/1998	South Africa v Wales - Minolta Loftus, Pretoria	Won	96-13	Replaced by Naka Drotské in the 67th minute
26	04/07/1998	South Africa v England - Norwich Park Newlands, Cape Town	Won	18-0	
27	18/07/1998	Australia v South Africa - Subiaco Oval, Perth	Won	13-14	
28	25/07/1998	New Zealand v South Africa - Athletic Park, Wellington	Won	3-13	
29	15/08/1998	South Africa v New Zealand - Kings Park, Durban	Won	24-23	Scored his fifth Test try
30	22/08/1998	South Africa v Australia - Ellis Park, Johannesburg	Won	29-15	
31	14/11/1998	Wales v South Africa - Wembley Stadium, London	Won	20-28	
32	21/11/1998	Scotland v South Africa - Murrayfield, Edinburgh	Won	10-35	
33	28/11/1998	Ireland v South Africa - Lansdowne Road, Dublin	Won	13-27	Replaced by Naka Drotské in the 12th minute
34	05/12/1998	England v South Africa - Twickenham, London	Lost	13-7	
35	08/06/2002	South Africa v Wales - Vodacom Park, Bloemfontein	Won	34-19	Replaced by Ollie le Roux in the 70th minute
36	15/06/2002	South Africa v Wales - Newlands, Cape Town	Won	19-8	
37	29/06/2002	South Africa v Argentina - PAM Brink Stadium, Springs	Won	49-29	Replaced by Daan Human in the 55th minute
38	20/07/2002	New Zealand v South Africa - WestpacTrust Stadium, Wellington	Lost	41-20	

39	27/07/2002	Australia v South Africa - The Gabba, Brisbane	Lost	38-27	Replaced by Delarey du Preez in the 71st minute
40	10/08/2002	South Africa v New Zealand - ABSA Stadium, Durban	Lost	23-30	
41	17/08/2002	South Africa v Australia - Ellis Park, Johannesburg	Won	33-31	Replaced by Ollie le Roux in the 62nd minute
42	09/11/2002	France v South Africa - Stade Vélodrome, Marseilles	Lost	30-10	
-	16/11/2002	Scotland v South Africa - Murrayfield, Edinburgh	Lost	21-6	Unused substitute
43	23/11/2002	England v South Africa - Twickenham, London	Lost	53-3	His last Test match - Replaced by Lukas van Biljon in the 54th minute

James played in 43 Test matches with 35 on the winning side and eight on the losing side - an impressive 81% wins. Only Adrian Garvey (86%) and Morné du Plessis (82%) have a better win ratio of all Springboks who played in 20 or more Tests.

He made 10 appearances in the Tri Nations, scoring two tries, and played in two Tests at the 1995 Rugby World Cup.

With 43 Test caps, he is the fourth-most capped Springbok hooker behind John Smit (111), Bismarck du Plessis (79) and Adriaan Strauss (66).

He is fourth on the list of tries scored by a hooker (5) with Bismarck du Plessis (11), John Smit (8) and Adriaan Strauss (6) the top try scorers for South Africa.

In his 8 years of International rugby, he played against 11 countries and against the British & Irish Lions.

James Dalton was born on 16 August, 1972 in Johannesburg.

JAMES DALTON - 15 TOUR MATCHES AS A SPRINGBOK					
	DATE	TEAMS AND VENUES	SA RESULT	SCORE	REMARKS
1	23/06/1994	King Country - Owen Delaney Stadium, Taupo	Won	10-46	
2	28/06/1994	Wellington - Athletic Park, Wellington	Won	26-36	
3	05/07/1994	Hanan Shield Districts - Fraser Park, Timaru	Won	19-67	
4	13/07/1994	Taranaki - Rugby Park, New Plymouth	Won	12-16	
5	16/07/1994	Waikato - Rugby Park, Hamilton	Won	17-38	
6	19/07/1994	Manawatu - Palmerston North	Won	21-47	
7	27/07/1994	Otago - Carisbrook, Dunedin	Lost	19-12	
8	02/08/1994	Bay of Plenty - Rotorua	Won	12-33	
9	26/10/1994	Wales 'A' - Rodney Parade, Newport	Won	13-25	
10	02/11/1994	Neath - The Gnoll, Neath	Won	13-16	
11	09/11/1994	Scotland 'A' - The Greenyards, Melrose	Lost	17-15	
12	15/11/1994	Scottish Select - Rubislaw Playing Fields, Aberdeen	Won	10-35	
13	22/11/1994	Pontypridd - Sardis Road, Pontypridd	Won	3-9	
14	03/12/1994	Barbarians - Lansdowne Road, Dublin	Lost	23-15	
15	23/11/1996	French Barbarians - Municipal Stadium, Brive	Lost	30-22